BEYOND THE FISH STICKER

Seeking a Deeper
Knowledge of God
and Ourselves

BENJAMIN SWIFT

a. Acorn Press

Published by Acorn Press
An imprint of Bible Society Australia
ACN 148 058 306 | Charity licence 19 000 528
GPO Box 4161
Sydney NSW 2001
Australia
www.acornpress.net.au | www.biblesociety.org.au

ISBN 978-0-647-53351-2

First published by Morning Star Publishing in 2019,
ISBN 978-0-648-45387-1

A catalogue record for this book is available from the National Library of Australia

Cover and text design and layout by John Healy

For my beautiful wife and daughters,
Suellen, Josie, Mikayla and Amelia.

To my loving parents, John and Beverley,
thanks for everything.

CONTENTS

Preface

I find it interesting how the comments of others, even people far removed from our inner circles, can become cemented in our minds, reasserting themselves in later years. I recall the words of a teacher and colleague from a number of years ago who referred to me as 'deep waters'. There may or may not be any truth to this metaphor, but either way it brings me to a place at which I'm sure many human beings arrive, a place where we are led to wonder about who we are and how to discern truth in a world full of delusion.

As the son of a preacher – an Anglican minister to be precise – I was always taught that my identity was in God, being made in his likeness and for the purpose of his glory. Maybe that's why the label P.K. (preacher's kid) never sat well with me. (Labels have never really sat well with me, especially if I have no influence on which ones are being forced upon me.)

But that's not what this book is about. If I really am 'deep waters', then what is it that floats around in the depths? Are there things embedded in our subconscious that explain the way we see the world? Some of history's greatest philosophical thought emerged as great thinkers such as Blaise Pascal, Martin Luther and C.S. Lewis responded to their innermost yearning for answers to life's big questions. I'm curious, and maybe you are too, about what these (and other) great thinkers have to say about the things of God and his universe. There are so many questions to explore.

I can still remember, as a young child, the very first time I left the safety of the shallow end of the pool for the deep. The fear and excitement accompanying that moment still occupies a place in my mind. The deep end can certainly be a scary place when you are used to the safety of the shallows. But just as we all need to move from milk to solid food in our younger years, our Christianity becomes richer as we move beyond the shallows and into the deep.

It is my hope that the thoughts and reflections in this book will allow you, the reader, to escape the shallows of worldly thought and be taken into deeper waters.

Introduction

As humanity seeks to find meaning in life, searching for the truth about who we are, it's difficult not to wonder in awe at the world and universe that surrounds us and to ask questions about God in the midst of this wonder.

But what is it that we find when we truly seek to know God? Can we, in reality, know God?

'I want to know his [God's] thoughts, the rest are details.'[1]

I recall, in my university years, purchasing a vivid poster of Einstein sharing these words and sticking it to my bedroom wall. Many of us are familiar with this famous quote, and Christians are often swift to use it to claim the great mind of Albert Einstein for Christianity. The truth, however, when the context of Einstein's quote is considered, is far from what it first may seem. According to an article from the Stanford Encyclopaedia of Philosophy, a more accurate rendition of Einstein's quote is, 'I want to know how God created this world. I'm not interested in this or that phenomenon, in the spectrum of this or that element. I want to know his thoughts, the rest are details.'[2] It has been suggested that Einstein used the term 'God' in exchange for 'the laws of the universe'. In this way, the laws of physics are represented as the 'thoughts of God'. What Einstein was suggesting was that he wasn't so much interested in experiments and the filling out of theories but rather in how the universe was created and exists from a mathematical standpoint.

---

1 Alice Calaprice, *The Expanded Quotable Einstein*, Princeton University Press, Princeton, 2000, p. 202.
2 Don A. Howard, *Einstein's Philosophy of Science*, Stanford Encyclopedia of Philosophy (Fall 2017 Edition), Edward N. Zalta (ed.), URL = <https://plato.stanford.edu/archives/fall2017/entries/einstein-philscience/>.

Putting Einstein's religious or philosophical stances aside, he does share a common thread with many who seek answers about such things as origins, existence, life, death and how everything in our universe works. From a Christian perspective, God has gifted humanity with what many like to think of as a complex mind and consciousness. It would be a redundant gift if we were not supposed to use it. Towards the end of the children's novel *Charlotte's Web*, Mr Zuckerman, farmer and owner of Wilbur, the pig seemingly surrounded by miraculous signs, suggests that maybe we are all surrounded by miracles on a daily basis but rarely have our eyes open enough to notice them.

It could be argued that it's not only life itself that's a miracle; it's that we are able to appreciate and reflect on it. What is it about humanity that allows us to consider life, not only from a biological perspective but from philosophical, anthropological and theological perspectives (to name a few)? If we are simply random by-products of natural selection, doesn't it seem a bit odd that we would care at all about the deep questions concerning who we are, both as living beings and in relation to a first cause of existence? I'm pretty confident my dog doesn't lie around contemplating these questions.

Perhaps that's why great children's novels such as *Charlotte's Web* are so powerful, because by animating animal characters with human traits such as reasoning, we can identify with them and in turn learn about ourselves. Wilbur the pig, a humble, childlike character, makes the following point, which gets to the heart of many debates between atheists and theists on the origin of creation:

> What do you mean less than nothing? I don't think there is any such thing as less than nothing. Nothing is absolutely the limit of nothingness. It's the lowest you can go. It's the end of the line. How can something be less than nothing? If there were something that was less than nothing, then

nothing would not be nothing, it would be something – even though it's just a very little bit of something. But if nothing is nothing, then nothing has nothing that is less than it is.[3]

Just as the Christian believes that faith is a gift from God, sustained by the ongoing work of the Holy Spirit, humanity's ability to reason is also a gift. It is what separates us from the animals, allowing us to contemplate meaning and truth. This is where the argument of the naturalist or humanist crumbles. If we are all sitting at a point in time in an ongoing process of natural selection, there would be no reason for the development of reason; it simply doesn't fit the requirements for the survival of the fittest. It would be ridiculous for me to be writing about this topic at all if the naturalist's humanistic reasoning is correct. In the words of C.S. Lewis:

> It is agreed on all hands that reason, and even sentience, and life itself are late comers in Nature. If there is nothing but Nature, therefore, reason must have come into existence by a historical process. And of course, for the Naturalist, this process was not designed to produce a mental behaviour that can find truth. There was no Designer, and indeed, until there were thinkers, there was no truth or falsehood. The type of mental behaviour we now call rational thinking or inference must therefore have been 'evolved' by natural selection, by the gradual weeding out of types less fitted to survive … But it is not conceivable that any improvement of responses could ever turn them into acts of insight, or even remotely tend to do so.[4]

It is only when the gift of faith is intertwined with the gift of reason that we can cast off the shackles of the naturalist's confined way of thinking. Only then can the miracles in life be seen in all their glory – that is, reflecting the glory of God the

---

3 E.B. White, *Charlotte's Web*, Harper and Brothers, New York, 1952, Chapter 4.
4 C.S. Lewis, *The Complete C.S. Lewis Signature Classics – Miracles*, HarperOne, Harper Collins Publishers, New York, 2002, p. 220.

Creator. After all, we have been made to relate to our Creator, who has revealed himself to us in ways that defy the logic of an existence limited to nature as science currently defines it.

While as followers of Christ we are called to faith, we are not called to ignorance. This is an important point. On more than one occasion in his letters, the Apostle Paul introduces his new ideas with the statement, 'We do not want you to be ignorant'.

Author Neil Cullan McKinlay suggests that it is impossible for humanity to comprehend the truth about who we are until God is acknowledged as the beginning and the end of all existence. It is for this reason that we need to study God as a means of knowing him from his revelation in Scripture.

With historical evidence supporting biblical accounts, we have no reason for reluctance in seeking to know what Scripture reveals to us about the reality of God, or at least the reality he chooses to reveal to us.

But the question remains, 'Just how much does God want us to know, and how much should be left to faith and humility?'

As we read through Scripture and meditate on what it is revealing to us, we soon come to comprehend that, while God provides his people with much insight into his character and the plan that has always existed for his people through Christ, there are many questions that remain unanswered or must be left to faith.

Leon Morris, a well-respected theologian, wisely suggests, 'There are many things that we would like to know, but the Bible was not written to gratify our curiosity. Rather it is intended to help us in our Christian lives, and for that the important thing is that we should be ready when the Lord comes'.[5]

God remains a hidden God in many ways. We cannot fully know him, and yet he has revealed himself to us in the created

---

5 Leon Morris, *The First and Second Epistles to the Thessalonians (Revised)*, Eerdmans, Grand Rapids MI, 1991, p. 142.

order and most clearly in the person of Christ. Perhaps this is why Martin Luther claimed to flee from the God who hides himself and toward the God who became human, revealing himself to us in the life of Christ.

Faith in God, it seems, is the inevitable resting place in which we must become childlike once again, humbling ourselves before the one who asks for our trust. This is why atheists will continue to find the message of the cross a stumbling block, because it will always require faith. As human beings, curiosity is innate, and we all want answers. For this reason, the faith that Christ demands can only live in us through the work of the Holy Spirit, a gift allowing us to see beyond reason and towards a present and future hope with our incomprehensible God.

Oh, the depth of the riches of the wisdom and knowledge of God! How unsearchable his judgements, and his paths beyond tracing out! (Rom 11:33)

It is the goal of this book, through a series of musings, to enable personal spiritual growth through a reasoned understanding of who we are as God's people in light of what he has revealed to us about himself, and what that means for our fragile yet significant lives, which depend on his very breath.

Throughout chapter 1, our understanding of what it means to be human is put under the microscope. Topics such as pain and suffering will help us to consider the alternative truths that we are presented with from the wider culture. As these are uncovered, we find that hope worth hoping for can be found in Christ alone.

Chapter 2 is a search for truth and meaning. Here, the insanity that often accompanies a humanity trying to usurp God's position is brought to light. Alternatively, we find that it is by taking on the mind of Christ, through the ongoing work of the Holy Spirit, that we find the only real path to sanity. Our goals in pursuing dreams and personal happiness at any cost are put into question. Instead, we learn that to gain life, we must be prepared to lose it for Christ's glory.

In chapter 3, the reasonableness of the Christian faith is explored. What is ultimate truth in light of Christ's exclusive claims about himself? Reason and the reasonableness of people are brought to examination. How do we give a reason for what we believe, and where does faith come into the equation? Through all of these things, we learn to interpret the complex world in which we live through the wisdom of Christ and the cross.

Chapter 4 asks the vexing question brought about by suffering: 'Does God really care?' Throughout this section the depth of God's love is explored. The truth about God's intimate and perfect love for his people, as ultimately revealed in the cross of Christ, is laid out.

Chapter 5 focuses on what it means to embrace and grow in the Christian faith. It is here that we will come face to face with a profound and challenging message, one that calls us to move well beyond superficial Christianity and worldly wisdom.

Finally, we will return to the original questions asked at the beginning of the book, reflecting on what it truly means to live a life rooted in the eternal truth of Christ.

It's time to jump in the deep end!

Philip said, 'Lord, show us the Father and that will be enough for us'.

Jesus answered: 'Don't you know me, Philip, even after I have been among you such a long time? Anyone who has seen me has seen the Father' (Jn 14:8–9).

1. Being God's Human Beings

Not so random

The question of what it is to be human is one that has surely entered the minds of any person who has the mental capacity to reflect on the deeper things of life. But just how far must we travel in our search for a satisfactory answer; an answer that we can confidently call truth or at least reality? Finding answers to such questions can and will take us in all sorts of directions, and so we need a starting point. Let's see what science has to say.

At a scientific level, humans, like all other animals, consist of cells, the very fabric of life. These cells work together to enable the physiological and biochemical processes required by the organism to take place as it lives in an environment that meets the conditions needed for life. The specific bundles of cells known as humans are, along with apes and lemurs, classified as mammals and belong to the order of primates – the highest level of mammal. They are first in the animal kingdom in brain development, with especially large cerebral hemispheres. That's right – humans have, in terms of the animal kingdom, relatively large brains.

But it's what drives these brains, beyond mere biological explanations, that should be of greater interest.

Science, despite being a discipline closely associated with logic, has nonetheless led people to strange places when it comes to finding answers about the human condition. In 1907, Duncan MacDougall, an American physician, conducted a bizarre investigation known as 'Weighing the Ghost'.[1] He actually attempted to measure the weight of the human soul. His investigation involved placing people literally on their death bed, enabling a difference in weight between the alive

1 Anne Rooney, *The Story of Psychology*, Arcturus, London, 2015, p. 29.

specimen and the dead specimen to be taken at the exact moment the soul was to hypothetically leave the body. Not surprisingly, nothing was really gained from these experiments.

Science as a discipline can teach us many things, but it has its limits. Humans are more than complex cellular organisms, and not everything about us can be tested and measured scientifically. Unless we are prepared to tackle the 'Who am I?' question at a psychological and spiritual level, rather than at a material level, something of crucial importance to the understanding of what it is to be human remains a mystery.

While it would be foolish to deny that genetics plays a role in many aspects of who we are, just as it does throughout the animal kingdom, it cannot explain why we, unlike other animals, have a consciousness that calls us into a place of reflection and a search for meaning. You will find no written accounts reflecting on the longings of the heart from the perspective of a lemur. There's just something higher about the human race, something that cannot be explained by including us purely as a piece of the evolutionary jigsaw puzzle.

There are many voices trying to flag down our attention, hoping to convince us that they have the keys to the vault holding the truth about who we are – voices of humanists, philosophers and religious teachers, among others.

Consider a thought from the Buddha: 'All that we are is the result of what we have thought. The mind is everything. What we think, we become.'[2]

But what is the basis for such a claim? If we choose to venture down this path, our sense of meaning lies completely with the self, and it seems that the self has been unable to truly satisfy its own desire for higher meaning. The truth about who we are must transcend ourselves. Denial is a powerful mental state, but surely, we can't deny that reality exists simply by thinking it into being something more palatable.

---

2 *Thoughts of the Buddha: 24 enlightened quotations for every day guidance*, Affirmations, Bellingen NSW, 2014. (quotes printed on individual cards)

Alternatively, Genesis 1:26 clearly illuminates the special creative intentions that God has for human beings, explaining why we are the way we are.

'Then God said, "Let us make mankind in our image, in our likeness, so that they may rule over the fish of the sea and the birds in the sky, over the livestock and all the wild animals, and over all the creatures that move along the ground."

McKinlay puts it this way:

> He gave his own reflection five senses to appreciate his beautiful creation. And with his own finger he delicately wrote his law of love on his little mirror as he breathed life into him. As the three persons love the eternal Godhead, so man was to image his Creator by loving God and his neighbour personally, perfectly and perpetually.[3]

It is exclusively through our understanding of who we are in relation to who God is that we come to comprehend what it means to be human. We have been gifted with the capacity to reflect the very nature of our Creator. Who we have become is often far from who we have been created to be, and perhaps that's why throughout history we have so widely missed the mark when it comes to answering the question of what it means to be human. The more we close our eyes and ears to all that Christ reveals to us about ourselves, the more we use our creative capacities to construct meaning from a source separated from truth and life itself.

Understanding the truth of what it is to be human means avoiding reducing ourselves to a complex clump of cells answerable only to our DNA and being convinced by philosophies that preach the death of God and the power of the self. Surely, it would be more rational to turn to a God who knows us better than we know ourselves – a God who has experienced what it is to be human.

---

[3] Neil Cullan McKinlay, *The Song of Creation and Other Contemplations*, Dragonwick, Goonellabah NSW, 2006, p. 23.

Everybody hurts

When it comes to the problem of trying to make sense of pain and suffering in this life, surely nobody has been without their own personal set of struggles. Perhaps that's why the country music scene has such a huge following of people who identify with the melancholy, story-telling lyrics of broken relationships and the struggles we all face in the changing seasons of our lives.

Has anyone on their journey through life not questioned how they have somehow arrived at this unforeseen, and possibly unbearable, destination that is the present? If we could only wind back the hands of time, correct the irreversible consequences of our naïve choices. The hole we sometimes find ourselves in may not be our intended situation, but nevertheless the machine that is Western society holds us tight in its grip. The worries of this world, of this life, seem to have us by the scruff. It can feel as though every time we try and fill some of our hole with a shovel full of soil, the world sends in a high-powered digging machine to take us deeper.

As the old saying, 'There's a fine line between pleasure and pain', suggests, the experiences of life can be perceived as pendulum-like, swinging us from emotion to emotion as our circumstances drag us from ecstasy to despair and everywhere in between. If we pour all of our energy into bringing this pendulum to a grinding holt, however, what will be the consequence? If we attempt to walk the fine line between pleasure and pain, placing ourselves in protective bubbles, will it lead to the exclusion of life itself?

If we turn to the book of Ecclesiastes and to Christian existentialists for advice, we begin to gain some interesting perspectives. The goal common to much of humanity, that of seeking personal happiness above all else through wealth, fame and physical pleasure, is likened to chasing the wind. The values of the common person are reduced to vanity.

Yet when I surveyed all that my hands had done and what

I had toiled to achieve, everything was meaningless, a chasing after the wind; nothing was gained under the sun (Eccl 2:11).

Time, wealth, possessions, popularity – all are potential idols that the world assures us maketh the person. How can we possibly seek to spend time with God, listening to his voice and leaning on his truth, if all of our time is spent chasing after the things that are here today and gone tomorrow?

The thirst for comfort, wealth and fame is unquenchable and consequently snuffs out the parts of life that point us to truth and meaning. Danish philosopher Søren Kierkegaard took this line of thinking to the extreme. It was said that Kierkegaard refused a parsonage, which would have brought him a steady income, left his fiancée and the chance of a settled family life and deliberately used his talent as a thinker to bring ridicule upon himself.[4] Why? Because he recognised that comfort, money and public approval are inferior values.

To anyone living in a modern, Western society, this way of thinking seems absurd; it goes against everything that the world has programmed our minds with since the day we left the womb. But then again, is it absurd to recognise the futile pursuits of the world for what they are, attempting to replace them with a way of living that actually awakens us to who we really are and who we have been created to be?

In relation to suffering, Karl Barth suggests, 'Participation in suffering means to suffer with Christ, to encounter God, as Jeremiah and Job encountered Him; to see Him in the tempest, to apprehend Him as Light in the darkness, to love Him when we are aware only of the roughness of His hand'.[5]

Whether we willingly plunge ourselves into suffering in the way that existentialists do or not, the reality still remains that to live is to experience both pleasure and pain. This is life. This

4 Robert Olson, *An Introduction to Existentialism*, Dover, New York, 2017, p. 2.
5 Karl Barth, *The Epistle to the Romans*, 6th edn, Oxford University Press, Oxford, translated by Edwyn Hoskyns, 1968, p. 301.

is a truth that cannot be avoided. The problem with pain and suffering is that we cannot avoid what is outside of our control. We must learn to play the cards dealt to us throughout our lives, knowing that life often deals us a losing hand.

Consider the phenomenon known as 'the butterfly effect'. As part of an idea used by physicists in chaos theory, the butterfly effect describes a minute alteration to the initial state of a physical system that can result in a large, significant difference to the state at a later time. The concept famously uses the exaggerated example of a butterfly flapping its wings in one country, only to cause a cyclone in another due to the initial environmental change caused by the beating of the wings.

In a sense, the butterfly effect can help us to understand the problem of pain, because life appears chaotic. It is chaotic in that outside factors such as other people, the natural world, financial instability and disease can be the cause of our suffering, and we have little to no control over how they will affect us personally and collectively. What we *do* have control over is how we will respond when bad things happen, not in the sense that we won't feel broken and torn apart, but in relation to who we turn to in order to make sense of life and its tribulations. It is here that, by the work of the Holy Spirit, we will see that only in Christ the perceived chaos is actually all under control; there is an endpoint where suffering will cease, and there is comfort in the refuge of our God.

Martin Luther was certainly subjected to his fair share of trials and tribulations and offers us the following thoughts: 'When left and forsaken of all men, in my highest weakness, in trembling, and in fear of death, when persecuted of the wicked world, then I felt most deeply the divine power which this name, Christ Jesus, communicated unto me.'[6]

As finite, frail human beings, we need to be aware of who

---

[6] Martin Luther, *The Tabletalk of Martin Luther*, Christian Focus, Scotland, 2003, p. 186.

we are and who God is, becoming wrapped in the one who is greater than ourselves.

> *Hear my cry, Oh God; listen to my prayer. From the ends of the earth I call to you, I call as my heart grows faint; lead me to the rock that is higher than I. For you have been my refuge, a strong tower against the foe. I long to dwell in your tent forever and take refuge in the shelter of your wings (Ps 61:1–4).*

Wherever I go, there I am

To better understand the problem of pain and suffering and why our only hope of refuge exists in God and not ourselves, we need to consider the part we all play. After all, one thing is for certain in this life: we cannot escape ourselves.

It is popular to hold that most people are basically good people. Well, at least that's the delusion many of us choose to live in. But it would be difficult for anyone to convincingly deny the fact that evil has a real presence in this world. One doesn't have to travel far through the pages of history to find extraordinarily cruel cases of evil.

Take communist Khmer Rouge leader Pol Pot, for example. In his time of political leadership, an estimated one-and-a-half to two million Cambodians died of starvation, execution, disease or exhaustion. Evil is at its most obvious in cases like these. But disturbingly, it can be found lurking in the hearts of every human being, as the inherited seed of our most ancient ancestors.

This is why, in his book *Deliver Us from Evil*, Christian apologist Ravi Zacharias suggests that evil is found not just where blood has been spilled; rather, it is found in the self-absorbed human heart.[7] The psalmist is in agreement:

> *For I know my transgressions, and my sin is always before me. Against you, you only, have I sinned and done what is evil in your sight, so that you are proved right when you*

---

7 Ravi Zacharias, *Deliver Us from Evil*, Thomas Nelson, Nashville TN, 1997.

> *speak and justified when you judge. Surely I was sinful at birth, sinful from the time my mother conceived me. Yet you desired faithfulness even in the womb; you taught me wisdom in that secret place (Ps 51:3–6).*

When most people contemplate the association of sin with humanity, they connect sin with behaviour rather than inherent nature. Descriptions such as those found in Jon Ronson's *The Psychopath Test* probably fit with more commonly accepted ideas about who should wear the sin label.[8] Psychiatrists often regard psychopaths as inhuman, relentlessly evil forces that are forever harming society. Surely in comparison, the average person can't be regarded as sinful?

In the year 1987, Mikhail Gorbachev released his book *Perestroika*, which proposed in detail his 'New Thinking for Our Country and the World'. Gorbachev, with seemingly the best intentions for his Soviet comrades and the human race in mind, proposed the following:

> Perestroika is giving socialism the most progressive forms of social organisation; it is the fullest exposure of the humanist nature of our social system in its crucial aspects – economic, social, political and moral.[9]

With this part of history now in the rear-view mirror, the question can be asked, 'Why didn't Perestroika succeed in creating a peaceful, thriving utopia for the masses?'

While many may suggest the answer to be complex, might not a better suggestion be that it failed due to its inability to account for the common thread of sin that can never be revolutionised away from the human condition?

The atheist view on sin has to be that it is non-existent, in that it is subjective, and I decide what is right and wrong. Atheist Richard Dawkins, in his book *The God Delusion*, asks,

---

8 Jon Ronson, *The Psychopath Test: A journey through the madness test*, Picador, London, 2012.
9 Mikhail Gorbachev, *Perestroika*, Harper and Row, New York, 1987, p. 35.

'What kind of ethical philosophy is it that condemns every child, even before it is born, to inherit the sin of a remote ancestor [Adam]?'[10] Atheists – and people with many other worldviews alike – struggle with the notion that we are all born with sin at the core of our nature.

So how did the human heart become this way? Could it be that the Sunday school stories about what went on in Eden were really profound lessons concerning the origins of inherent human sin?

Martin Luther confessed that it is evident in Scripture that all human beings come originally from one man, Adam, and from this individual, by means of birth, the fall, guilt and sin come along with it and are inherited.

As described by systematic theologian Louis Berkhof, the essence of Adam's sin lay in the fact that he placed himself in opposition to God, refusing to subject his will to the will of God and to have God determine the course of his life.[11] To put it another way, Adam desired to be like God and so, in pride, defied his Creator.

Many years have passed since the writings of Genesis, but as the saying goes, 'There's no such thing as the evolution of the human spirit'. Blinded as we are by the pride at the heart of our sinful nature, Jesus clearly lays before us some harsh truths about our inability to recognise the person in the mirror.

'Why do you look at the speck of sawdust in your brother's eye and pay no attention to the plank in your own eye?' (Mt 7:3)

The truth about sinful nature is that it is inherent in all of us. We can be transformed, however, by the knowledge that although we are dead in sin, we are made alive in Christ.

Dr Leon Morris recognised this when he wrote:

> To put it bluntly and plainly, if Christ is not my Substitute,

---

10 Richard Dawkins, *The God Delusion*, Transworld, London, 2006, p. 285.
11 Louis Berkhof, *Systematic Theology*, Eerdmans, Grand Rapids MI/ Cambridge UK, 1996, p. 221.

I still occupy the place of a condemned sinner. If my sins and my guilt are not transferred to him, if he did not take them upon himself, then surely they remain with me. If he did not deal with my sins, I must face their consequences. If my penalty was not borne by him, it still hangs over me. There is no other possibility.[12]

None of us can shift the blame for the sin that we personally bring into this world. We, as free people, have the ability to make choices and must live with the consequences of the wrong decisions of both ourselves and others. Here the relationship between evil, sin and suffering become painfully apparent, with world history highlighting time and again what twisted hearts are capable of enacting – even to the point of crucifying the Son of God.

Naked before God

You would, I believe, struggle to find a more profound text capable of explaining the broken state of our world and the condition of humanity than Genesis chapters 2 and 3. In the garden of Eden, human beings first did what they have continued to do ever since. Creating God in their own image, they continue to live in the delusion of their self-constructed truths.

In *Being Human*, Peter Vardy suggests that postmodernism has led us to lose confidence in the very concept of truth, and as such its impact has been devastating.[13] The Western world suffers from the perceived lack of meaning brought about by the so-called 'death of God'. Humanism has become aligned with the idea that human beings result from a universe evolving through random events with no meaning. Could this lack of real purpose lie at the heart of many of modern society's problems?

12 Leon Morris, *The Cross in the New Testament*, Eerdmans, Grand Rapids MI/Cambridge UK, 1999, p. 410.

13 Peter Vardy, *Being Human: Fulfilling genetic and spiritual potential*, Darton, Longman and Todd, London, 2003, p. 95.

Putting the broken condition of the world aside, there is still an important truth that we need to confront. God is God and we are not. There is no religious or philosophical construct within which we can work to save ourselves and become right with God. After all, we are all born with an innate desire for a bite of that forbidden fruit that leads to death, as the story goes. Fortunately, Jesus reminds us in Luke's Gospel that what's impossible for humanity is possible with God. In other words, God has a way to make things right.

John Stott, in his book *The Cross of Christ*, exposes the human heart well. He suggests:

> *We insist on paying for what we have done. We cannot stand the humiliation of acknowledging our bankruptcy and allowing somebody else to pay for us. The notion that this somebody else should be God himself is just too much to take. We would rather perish than repent, rather lose ourselves than humble ourselves.*[14]

Despite any desperate attempts we make, we cannot hide from God. We can't hide by clinging to so called 'alternative truths' that deny our humanity and God's divinity. We, like Adam and Eve, cannot hide and avoid standing naked before God.

But thank God that we can be confident to stand naked before God with the knowledge that we are justified in Christ, not ourselves. We can take heart in the truth that humanity's saviour is not humanity.

Hope worth hoping for

World renowned scientist Stephen Hawking was once asked to share his opinion on the divisive issue of euthanasia. His well-documented answer was, 'The victim should have the right to end his life, if he wants. But I think it would be a great mistake. However bad life may seem, there is always something

---

14 John Stott, *The Cross of Christ*, Inter-Varsity, Nottingham, 2006, p. 191.

you can do and succeed at. While there's life, there is hope'.[15]

While there may be some truth in this response, it raises other questions such as, 'Hope in what?'

Not so long ago, in a city not so far away, Louis Theroux conducted a documentary-style investigation into the decisions that people make after being informed by medical specialists that they, or a close loved one, has very little time, if any, to live.[16] This may be due to cancer, or any other cruel disease or medical situation requiring life support. The findings of the investigation indicated that in the majority of cases, patients or next of kin were willing to do whatever it takes, no matter how distressing and painful, for hope of a medical miracle, thus avoiding death for whatever short amount of extra time they could gain. Very rarely, and seemingly miraculously, patients on artificial life-support do awake, but sadly for the majority of patients, their hope goes in vain.

Nonetheless, hope seems to be imbedded into our DNA. But where we choose to direct our hope remains widely varied.

So, what hope is worth hoping for?

Should we grasp hold of the hope offered by Eastern teachings such as Hinduism? This would at least give us hope that if we live rightly according to its teachings, we may move one step closer to *Moksha,* thus becoming one with Brahman (the ultimate reality) where we belong. But then again, if things don't go so well, all we can expect is to be reborn into a lower form of caste life. Hope in this case falls on us. That's a lot of pressure.

---

15 'Stephen Hawking: Terminally ill patients should have the right to die', *The Evening Standard*, 17 September 2013, 'Terminally https://www.standard.co.uk/news/health/stephen-hawking-terminally-ill-patients-should-have-the-right-to-die-8822083.html. His quote is a response to issues surrounding terminally ill patients and their right to die.

16 BBC documentary presenter Louis Theroux, in an episode called 'Choosing Death' from a series 'Altered States', investigated California's right to die laws for terminally ill patients and those who are in pain but not terminally ill. The documentary was broadcast on 18 November 2018.

Hope in a world rife with suffering must offer a way of dealing with the unbearable. We could dedicate our lives to the avoidance of suffering by following the Buddhist teaching, extinguishing all desire through eliminating all human cravings. But then why would we want to eliminate craving the very things that God made us to crave? Things such as love for one and other, or the desire to be amid the beauty of creation itself.

Make no mistake. There are things in this life worth hoping for. We're all aware of the clichéd longings of potential Miss Universe contestants as they 'hope for world peace'. An end to war and the suffering surrounding war, a solution for the effects of climate change, the eradication of domestic violence – these are aims worthy of our hope, but in the end, they cannot satisfy the deep desire in us for an ultimate hope, a hope that satisfies the questions that reach into the realm of eternity.

Ultimately, Christian hope rests on the fact that everything will be made, and is being made, perfectly new through Christ, including our relationship with God. As Christopher Wright suggests, 'Revelation rolls back the curse to welcome the unhindered presence of God with the simple, world-changing words, "No longer will there be any curse" (Rev 22:3).'[17]

But if hope worth hoping for is to be found in Christ, then how can we be assured of this hope?

The truth as expressed in God's word, the Bible, assures those who belong to God that the hope we have in Christ will not go in vain. It is a rock we can build our lives on. Assurance in hope is thus dependent on the gift of faith. It cannot be accepted in any other way.

In this life we will place our hope in many things, all of which contribute to shape our lives. The question that will define our lives, though, comes down to, 'What will be the source of our ultimate hope, and in what truth will our hope

---

[17] Christopher J.H. Wright, *The God I don't Understand: Reflections on Tough Questions of Faith,* Zondervan, Grand Rapids MI, 2008, p. 211.

rest?' While I long for my children to live in a world where freedom, beauty and love rule, it is only through Christ that this is ultimately possible. The good news can be found exclusively in the ultimate hope that has been made possible through Christ alone. This is a hope worth hoping for, a sure and certain hope – a living hope.

> *Praise be to the God and Father of our Lord Jesus Christ! In his great mercy he has given us new birth into a living hope through the resurrection of Jesus Christ from the dead, and into an inheritance that can never perish, spoil or fade … kept in heaven for you (1 Pet 1:3–4).*

The immortal mortals

This hope worth hoping for is one that can drastically alter our perspective on reality and should be reflected on in view of our own lives and the lives of those we connect with.

I have a vivid recollection of a situation in which I found myself reflecting, once again, on the deep things of life. It was during a boxing class that I first heard the tragic news of the death of a man I used to partner up with in training. He had quite suddenly died of brain cancer. I didn't know a lot about this man, except that he was only about sixty years of age and that he had dedicated much of his time in life to learning and teaching martial arts.

Hearing this news stirred up my thinking about the things of life and death yet again. We all dedicate our lives to a whole range of pursuits, but in the end, what do any of them really mean? Does most of what we do mean anything at all? One thing that stands out at funerals is the general belief that each person, once pronounced dead, is considered to have been the greatest person to ever have lived, and that it seems important in some respect for the person to be able to live on, whether in our hearts and minds or simply on a well-worded inscription in a graveyard.

What is it about humanity that makes us obsessed with living on, or to put it another way, with immortality?

Perhaps you're familiar with Irene Cara's song *Fame*,[18] in which she claims she will live forever, calling everyone to remember her name. Lyrics such as these just might sum up why we in the West are so caught up in fame. Do we really believe that through fame we can live forever? We've all seen the legacy of rock stars such as Prince being kept alive by the power of the media, but how does Prince himself benefit from this approach to achieving immortality? He's dead!

While there are many religious beliefs and teachings about immortality, for now, let's focus on what science has to offer. Charles Darwin, through his theory of evolution by means of natural selection and survival of the fittest, teaches us that we can live on through the passing on of our genes. In other words, we have the potential to achieve immortality through reproduction – an ability that is shared throughout the animal kingdom.

Take, for instance, lions. A lion pride consists of a group of closely related females and a smaller group of separately interrelated males, present for a shorter time. When a new male enters the pride and earns his right to take over the pride, he kills the young cubs fathered by the previous males. Why? I believe Darwin would argue that he is playing his role in the survival of the fittest and passing on his genetic information. You could say he is living on through his genes.

This logic isn't exclusive to the animal kingdom. People have been reproducing their way to immortality for as long as history has been recorded, especially when it comes to royalty. The film Braveheart has a classic line that highlights the importance to a king for his bloodline to continue. When the cruel King Edward the Longshanks was approaching his final breath, Queen Isabella whispers in his ear, 'You see? Death

---

18 Michael Gore and Dean Pitchford, *Fame*, RSO, 1980. Performed by Irene Cara for the film *Fame*.

comes to us all. But before it comes to you, know this: your blood dies with you. A child who is not of your line grows in my belly. Your son will not sit long on the throne. I swear it'.[19]

Death does come to us all. True immortality, that's another question altogether, bloodline or no bloodline.

What then can we learn from the Christian Scriptures about death? The writer of Ecclesiastes reflects:

> *Surely the fate of human beings is like that of the animals; the same fate awaits them both: as one dies, so dies the other. All have the same breath; humans have no advantage over animals. Everything is meaningless. All go to the same place; all come from dust, and to dust all return (Eccl 3:19–20).*

This gloomy reflection provides us with a reality check as to who we are. Human beings are not God. We are not immortal, and no attempts we make can change that truth.

Thankfully the Scriptures don't leave it at that. There is a way that our thirst for immortality can be satisfied. This is what lies at the heart of the good news of the Gospel message.

> *When the perishable has been clothed with the imperishable, and the mortal with immortality, then the saying that is written will come true: 'Death has been swallowed up in victory.' 'Where, O death is your victory? Where, O death is your sting?' The sting of death is sin, and the power of sin is the law. But thanks be to God! He gives us the victory through our Lord Jesus Christ (1 Cor 15:54–56).*

When Jesus was dying on the cross between two convicted criminals, the following message of hope was given.

> *One of the criminals who hung there hurled insults at him: 'Aren't you the Messiah? Save yourself and us!' But the other criminal rebuked him. 'Don't you fear God,' he said, 'since you are under the same sentence? We are punished justly, for we are getting what our deeds deserve. But this man has done*

---

19 Quote from the Mel Gibson film Braveheart, Icon Entertainment International, The Ladd Company, USA, 1995.

> *nothing wrong.' Then he said, 'Jesus, remember me when you come into your kingdom.' Jesus answered him, 'Truly I tell you, today you will be with me in paradise' (Lk 23:39–43).*

In the end, we can choose to put our hope in a vast array of things but the only true way to immortality requires us to enter through what Jesus referred to as 'the narrow gate' (Mt 7:13–14). What Christ achieved on the cross gives us an exclusive hope, in that we mere mortals can receive the gift of immortality through his grace.

Falling from Graceland

While living in God's grace is certainly our only hope of an eternity in his presence, is our hope assured?

The whole concept of 'falling from grace' has found itself in the centre of many Christian debates throughout the centuries. It refers to a person who at one time lived under God's grace, only to fall away to a state of God's condemnation. This whole concept rattles around in my mind because it infers that a person can at one time be a follower of Christ, only to reject this calling and deny the work of the Holy Spirit. A Lutheran pastor I know once likened this to giving God, and therefore his gift of grace, the proverbial finger. Obviously if we start journeying down this road, seeking to find answers where answers may not be found, we come to the hurdle of what it means to be God's elect.

People like to suggest that questions concerning Christian election and predestination are not worth getting too obsessed with, as in the end only God knows the answer, and the whole subject can become divisive. The problem is that our understanding of predestination impacts our ability to tackle the question, 'Can a person who is truly elect in Christ, having been transformed by the Holy Spirit, reject God, never to live under grace again?'

Lutheran pastor Friedemann Hebart suggests that the gift

of grace, made possible through what Christ has done, exists for all of humanity, as all have been chosen by God. It is the refusal of this gift that leads to the rejection of those who turn their back on God. God doesn't cause human opposition, even though he foresees it. According to the Formula for Concord:

> The reason why all who hear the Word do not come to faith and therefore receive the greater damnation is not that God did not want them to be saved. It is their own fault because they heard the Word of God not to learn but only to despise, blaspheme, and ridicule it, and they resisted the Holy Spirit who wanted to work within them.[20]

While this helps us to understand how God's grace can be rejected, it doesn't answer the question of whether grace can be rejected following a person's sincere willingness to let the Spirit work within their hearts.

What we can hold on to is the clear teaching throughout the Scriptures of God's ultimate control. Those who truly belong to Christ will not fall from grace; rather, Christ will ensure that they will be heirs to his eternal kingdom as adopted sons and daughters.

Perhaps one of the most important passages in the Scriptures that helps us to address this concern can be found in John 10:27–30:

> *Jesus said, 'My sheep listen to my voice; I know them, and they follow me. I give them eternal life, and they shall never perish; no one will snatch them out of my hand. My Father, who has given them to me, is greater than all; no one can snatch them out of my Father's hand. I and the Father are one.'*

In these words, Jesus makes it clear that those who belong to him can feel secure in the knowledge that they will not fall from grace, but rather be held onto in such a way that nothing

---

20 Hebart Friedemann, *One in the Gospel: The Formula of Concord for our day*, 2nd edn, Openbook, Howden SA, 2000, p. 148.

can separate them from him.

While the comfort and security of this truth is something that the Christian can wrap themselves up in for eternity, it still leaves us with the question, 'What about those who claim to have had faith and accepted Christ, but have now turned their backs on God?'

There have been many stories of pastors and devout church members who have renounced their faith, changed faith, turned to atheism or humanism or given up on life altogether. I have read stories of several famous, influential people who have dabbled in Christianity, only to fall away and follow the next path. While I suspect these are the types of stories that lead to the whole idea of 'falling from grace', only God will ever know the truth about the inner workings of each individual. I therefore believe it is wise for all of us to refrain from making any judgements regarding 'the sheep and the goats'.

What we have discovered on our journey so far is that while we continue to live in a world of broken, sinful people, pain and suffering will be an unavoidable part of our reality. The good news is that we can place our hope in something worth hoping for: a hope that can never be taken away. Those who live in God's grace will be held ever so tightly in the eternal hands of the Almighty.

For all have sinned and fall short of the glory of God, and are justified freely by his grace through the redemption that came by Christ Jesus (Rom 3:23-24).

2. Thinking about Thinking

Throughout life there will surely be many more questions than answers. These questions are the seeds of existentialist thinking, driving us to seek truth and meaning and discover what it means to live as a human being.

If you're anything like me, you will at some point in time have found yourself bewildered by the pursuits of humanity. Maybe I'm just cynical, but I find many of the activities that we hold up in worship to be, well, kind of ridiculous.

In the Western world, sports stars are held up as modern-day warrior gods; heroes destined for an eternal legacy. How else could we justify paying these individuals higher wages than brain surgeons? Take a step back and think about golf for a moment: millions of dollars dedicated to hitting small white balls into small holes in the grass with metal sticks!

Why else would we open our minds to the wisdom of pop stars as they spray insults about the greed of politicians while flying in their own private jets to record lip-sync sessions on commercial TV?

Now, I'm not for a moment claiming self-immunity to these bizarre behavioural patterns. But I am finding myself identifying more and more with the words in Ecclesiastes, 'This too is meaningless, a chasing after the wind'.

There may be some truth to Lady Gaga's suggestion that we were all born this way, but I believe the answers to our human condition can be better found in Genesis. Here we find the fall of humanity; the original seed of our desire to be our own god.

For God knows that when you eat from it your eyes will be opened, and you will be like God, knowing good and evil (Gen 3:5).

It is here in the original paradise called Eden that the desire to be like God sent us into a world of self-serving, people-worshiping pursuits, all of which equate to chasing the wind. We hear it over and over again, nothing is impossible for the person who follows their dreams, believing that they can achieve anything without limits. God's Word, however, is our constant reminder that we do have limits. We may convince ourselves that the infinite can be grasped by finite human hands but with every person's dying breath we should be reminded that eternity belongs to God alone.

To put it another way: 'One may best describe the fundamental project of the human reality in saying that man is the being who projects to be God... [and] God represents the permanent limits in terms of which man understands his being.'[1]

The humans must be crazy

One of my all-time favourite opening movie scenes is in an old but continually relevant film, *The Gods Must be Crazy*. The writers of this scene perceptively compare the contrasting life-styles of an isolated, ancient tribe of the Kalahari Bushmen to that of so-called modern civilisation.

Within a few minutes, it becomes obvious that the social and cultural progress of the modern person has in fact led to the evolution of a higher order of insanity. Let's be honest. Humanity in all its wisdom has consistently made life more complicated, fast-paced and self-serving with every passing decade.

I find it interesting that particularly in the workplace, research has proven beyond a doubt that we need to rest. But just how effectively do we cater for this fundamental human need within the workforce? For those working in the field of Christian education, for example – a world I am well-accustomed to – it's not uncommon for staff to begin the morning with a devotion, taking a short time to step back from

---

[1] Olson, *Introduction to Existentialism*, p. 59.

the world's frantic pace to rest in Christ. But while this is a well-intentioned thing, it often seems that the 'Amen' ending is synchronised with downloading the daily agenda for what needs to be achieved. Surely we can all see the irony of such a practice?

Unfortunately, when it comes to the ways in which we often live our lives, examples such as this are just the tip of the iceberg, while a much larger mass of stupidity lurks beneath the surface, evading our attention as it threatens to sink us like a human Titanic.

People, however, have not been created with stupidity in mind. In fact, as recorded in Genesis 1:26, God said, *'Let us make mankind in our image, in our likeness, so that they may rule over the fish of the sea and the birds of the sky, over the livestock and all the wild animals, and over all the creatures that move along the ground.'*

But it seems from the moment humanity sought to be their own gods, determined to go their own way, self-serving insanity has led the way.

When God warned people from the very beginning that if they were to turn their backs on him that they would surely die (Gen 3:3), did we ever conceive that the attrition of our wisdom and sanity would be a part of the dying process?

We don't need to travel far into our past to find classic examples to highlight the insanity of humanity. The tobacco industry and its assault on our species is a case in point. It would be fair to say that for some time, the effects of smoking on health were not completely understood. But as time passed and suspicions were confirmed by science, insanity kicked into its highest gear. In the knowledge that the tobacco industry was a death machine in motion, the response of many so-called civilized and sophisticated people was to continue to support the industry as it continued to support the economic desires of the collective. The statistics of this insanity are mind-blowingly sad. 'Globally, tobacco use killed 100 million people in the 20th century, much more than all deaths in World Wars I and II combined. Tobacco-related deaths will number around 1 billion in the 21st century if current smoking patterns continue.[2]

The insanity of humanity could be explicitly demonstrated from a number of angles. We could analyse our part in global environmental issues such as climate change, or zero in on our obsession for fashion and celebrity as they dictate the 'new black' for our lives. But if we just take the time to step back and reflect on ourselves, what will we find? What drives us to take up residence in such an unquestioning world of blind insanity?

The answer can only be found in the one who knows us because he created us; in the Creator, in whom our purpose needs to be regrafted. We have surely lost our way, but thanks be to Christ who is 'The Way'; the narrow path to sanity.

It is in Christ that we are able to see clearly just how intertwined with the insanity of the world we have become, but it's also in Christ that we receive through grace the gift of hope; a way to walk in truth.

> *But everything exposed by the light becomes visible – and everything that is illuminated becomes a light. That is why it is said: 'Wake up O sleeper, rise from the dead, and Christ will shine on you.' Be very careful, then, how you live – not as unwise but as wise (Eph 5:13–15).*

Of course, we must be prepared for the fact that to the insane, sanity will always appear to be insanity; wisdom will always appear to be foolishness. Christ warned us of such things. The path of following Christ may shine brightly to the illuminated mind but will remain hidden to the mind of those who continue to walk in darkness. Christianity does not provide us with a smooth ride in this life and will not allow us to live as one with the world. Insanity and sanity living side by side in a human mind will only lead to conflict and breakdown.

---

2 The Tobacco Atlas, http://tobaccoatlas.org/topic/smokings-death-toll/

There can only be two choices. We may take on the mind of Christ or take on the mind of those who have rejected Christ. No new, easier way can be constructed that exists in reality.

C.S. Lewis knew this well. Consider his words:

> If Christianity was something we were making up, of course we could make it easier. But it is not. We cannot compete, in simplicity, with people who are inventing religions. How could we? We are dealing with Fact. Of course anyone can be simple if he has no facts to bother about.[3]

It turns out that it's actually not the gods who must be crazy, but rather the ways of humanity. But without the Holy Spirit to expose our futile thinking, we cannot and will not, fully comprehend the insanity with which we live. Ultimately, to live outside of a relationship with our Creator is insane. It is to walk a path that leads us away from our very purpose in being and away from life. To gain life, we must be prepared to lose it; to live as fools for Christ in an insane world.

Theological shrink syndrome

> Don't ever let someone tell you that you can't do something. Not even me. You got a dream, you gotta protect it. When people can't do something themselves, they're gonna tell you that you can't do it. You want something, go get it. Period.[4]

This quote, taken from the book and subsequent motion picture, *The Pursuit of Happyness*, could well be what lies at the core of the postmodern worldview held by much of today's society. You don't have to travel far in daily life to find such sentiments repeatedly echoed. In fact, you only need travel as far as your TV remote and tune in to any number of reality shows dominating our screens. 'Stay true to yourself,' they say. 'This won't be the last we hear about you; just keep positive and

---

3 Lewis, *Complete C.S. Lewis*, p. 90.
4 Quote from the film *The Pursuit of Happyness*, Columbia Pictures Corporation, Relativity Media, Escape Artists, 2006.

follow your dreams. Don't let anybody get in your way.'

While this all sounds positive and may feel good, even right (while the delusion lasts), where has this way of thinking come from? Since when is our ultimate goal to pursue dreams and personal happiness at any cost?

I suggest that the roots of this way of thinking grew from the teachings of those who have sought to bring about the death of God from our understanding of life. One well-known father in this school of thought is Nietzsche. For him, the only self-worth really existing was the self of the 'Overman', the one who has risen above the conventional herd and has fashioned himself. He suggests that only a few are capable of this, because most of us have been constructed by the conventional language of our age and society.[5]

To rise above the herd, under the power of the self, requires a person to delve into the subconscious so as to overcome personal shortcomings and problems from the past, making positive steps towards fulfilling personal desires as dreams are chased and stumbling blocks broken down. It's here that we enter the realm of psychology.

Possibly the most well-known of psychologists, the cigar-smoking, silver-bearded Sigmund Freud, founder of psychoanalysis, believed and suggested that humanity's deepest problems can be dealt with by talking them through. He saw that through the process of conversing, we can come to recognise the real problem in which all of our problems are rooted: us. Freud also believed that a person, having acknowledged themselves as the centre of their problems, has the potential to rescue themselves – and thus fails to account for our inherent sinful nature and need of a transcendent saviour.

Those who claim Christianity as objective truth can't have it both ways. We can't claim that we seek the narrow path while

---

5 James W. Sire, *The Universe Next Door*, 5th edn, IVP Academic, Downers Grove IL, 2009, p. 227.

aligning ourselves with philosophies that deny our need for a saviour outside of ourselves, pointing us towards a personal pursuit for self-fulfilment. Consider the words of Jesus in his Sermon on the Mount. What contrasting words in light of postmodernist thinking.

> *'Blessed are the poor in spirit, for theirs is the kingdom of heaven. Blessed are those who mourn, for they will be comforted. Blessed are the meek, for they will inherit the earth. Blessed are those who hunger and thirst for righteousness, for they will be filled.... Blessed are those who are persecuted because of righteousness, for theirs is the kingdom of heaven' (Mt 5:3–6, 10).*

Interestingly, the things in which Christ calls us blessed are the very things that often send us knocking at the door of modern psychology.

When the positive view of human capacity, on view in most forms of modern psychology, makes its mark on modern theology, the message of the cross is watered down, and the serving of self prevails. This is because the worldview brought about by psychology in the absence of accurate biblical theology is based on the belief that human beings are primarily the product of their DNA code, naturally selected by chance in the process of the survival of the fittest; a notch on the evolutionary timeline.

Gary Gilley, in his book, *This Little Church Went to Market*, provides the following insight:

> Psychology, being man-centred, has as its highest goal the happiness of the individual. This is the foundation for the current emphasis on felt need. If mankind's greatest goal is his own happiness, then all other things in life, including God, become a means to secure that happiness … This worldview is completely at odds with the biblical worldview. Since this is true, to offer God or salvation as the means whereby our felt needs are satisfied is a perversion

of biblical teaching at best, and more likely a false gospel.[6]

It would be unwise to ignore the fact that there have been many important and beneficial discoveries in the areas of neuroscience and psychology. For the Christian, the important consideration is how to harmonise and apply the positive aspects of these discoveries in light of biblical teaching. The gospel message must never be compromised, nor the biblical view of who we are as people created through and for Christ. As I once heard a Lutheran pastor suggest to a group of primary aged students, 'It's impossible to pick yourself up in your own strength. Just take hold of your ankles and give it a try.'

Reality check

Human beings, while striving constantly to be God, end up existing in a state of anxiousness. We are endlessly faced with the reality that we can never become the true God. We may suppress this knowledge, bury it deep in our self-constructed denial, but we can never escape the moral law written permanently on our hearts. It is God who defines divinity and truth. It is exclusively he who holds the keys to the shackles of death; salvation exists in Christ alone. Therefore, those who want to play at being God remain haunted by the limits of their own humanity.

It is for this reason that Kierkegaard – possibly the father of existentialist thinking – believed that humans can only desire the eternal fullness that God alone possesses. We can only hold to the uncontrolled, unpredictable pleasures and pains of this finite life.[7]

No one can comprehend what goes on under the sun. Despite all their efforts to search it out, no one can discover its meaning. Even if the wise claim they know, they cannot really comprehend it (Eccl 8:17).

---

6 Gary Gilley, *This Little Church – Omnibus Edition*, EP Books, Darlington UK, 2014, p. 61-62.

7 Olson, *Introduction to Existentialism*, p. 60.

Surely the only way out of the existentialist conundrum can be found in the one who is both fully human and fully divine: the Christ. He, having intimate knowledge of all that it means to be human and to be all powerful and unlimited, as only God is, provides us with the narrow path to salvation. For this reason, in dying to self we gain true, eternal life in Christ.

Salvation is found in no one else, for there is no other name under heaven given to mankind by which we must be saved (Acts 4:12).

Undoubtedly for most of us, life will continue to serve up times to laugh, times to cry and seasons for everything under the sun. But these experiences can help us to dig deeper into what it all means, seeking the truth about who we are as limited creatures.

Perhaps we should stop chasing the wind and start resting in Christ.

3. Truth, Reason and Faith

How can I sleep when so torn deep within?
With each blessing a curse seems to blacken each win.
Is it that ignorance is where hides my bliss?
Should I seek my denial, betray truth with a kiss?
Or should I let fire burn deep in my soul,
Let the flames light desire, let it stir in the coals?
Should my mind walk a straight path shared by truth's
lonely sound?
Will my courage be turned as illusions abound?
And so, as I peer through the darkness of night,
Will I once again sleep, holding tight to truth's light?

There can, by definition, only be one truth. Either God's word is the truth or we followers of Christ are to be pitied more than all others (see 1 Cor 15:14–19).

We all have the freedom to believe whatever we like, but that doesn't alter what is ultimately true. For this reason, the question needs to be asked, 'What is the truth?'

'I am the way and the truth and the life. No one comes to the Father except through me' (Jn 14:6).

These words of Jesus are very exclusive and, if true, have consequences well worth our consideration. As Pascal once expressed:

> Christianity cannot be proved conclusively by reason, but neither can it be disproved. If it turns out that Christianity is true, we have everything to gain; but if it's false, we have nothing to lose. We should accept the inevitable risk of faith, and gamble on the truth of Christianity.[1]

While Pascal makes a clever point, the value of contemplating

---

1 Colin Chapman, *The Case for Christianity*, Lion, Oxford UK, 1981, p. 169.

the reasonableness of our faith is undeniable and can only serve to strengthen our ability to always give a reason for the faith we hold to (1 Pet 3:15). But let's firstly take a step back and put reason itself under the microscope.

Reason for reason

Historically speaking, the Age of Reason that occurred in the eighteenth century acknowledged a new birth in the way humanity viewed itself, the pursuit of knowledge and the universe. It came at a time in history when the risk of being labelled a heretic and burned alive at the stake for having new questions, ideas and opinions had become a thing of the past. It was during this period of history that people began to place their intellect on a pedestal, embracing an exaggerated perception of the perfection of humanity based on reason and clear thinking.

But just how reasonable are people? Are we even capable of true reason, or is our ability to reason with others always tainted by our own view of the world – a view most often based on our personal experience and desire for a particular version of truth?

John Calvin once suggested that 'the fantasy of the human being is a factory that works ceaselessly to make idols'.[2] He makes a valid point. So many of the things held up by people in worship are merely products of our own desires and imaginations, worship of creation rather than the Creator. There are endless idols to be made, and we can see their evolution correlate with the culture of the day. But ultimately, it is human reason in the absence of Christ that drives all idols into being.

With this in mind, is it at all possible for individuals holding to differing worldviews to effectively debate their differences of opinion based on reason? It does seem highly improbable, for

---

2 John Calvin, *Institutes of the Christian Religion*, 1.11.8; cf. 1.5.12.

example, that debaters bringing specific presuppositions to an argument could ever alter their opponent's view based on reason alone. For surely, their reasoning would stand in contradiction to a mind encased by a differing set of presuppositions.

So why do Christians, atheists, philosophers and scientists bother at all about presenting reason-based opinions to those who from the outset will be unlikely to shift their stance at all? For Christians who base their reasoning on the reality that God exists, and of Christ being who he claimed himself to be, any argument founded on alternative reasoning will be seen as one built on false foundations. Correspondingly, humanists in denial of the existence of a divine creator will discard any reasoning based on Scriptures as unauthoritative delusion. Surely you can see the problem here.

Some of the greatest debates that have occurred in recent history have been between the 'New Atheists' and Christians, particularly those holding solid scientific credentials to prop up their credibility in the halls of academia. Debates between respected minds such as Hitchens and Dawkins (in the atheist corner) and McGrath and Lennox (in the Christian corner) come to mind. But if you take a step back and observe these exchanges from the outside, what you will find is not an open-minded battle for the most reasonable argument but rather a host of people seeking confirmation bias on either side.

Confirmation bias is a powerful force in the development of our personal worldviews. As we enter life's many arenas of competing versions of truth and the many reasons given to support these truths, we prove to be highly capable creatures when it comes to opening our eyes and ears to whatever reason confirms our already predetermined points of view.

But is this a good or bad thing?

Surely it can only be a good thing if the bias being confirmed is based on a truth that aligns with reality. Sadly, and contrary to popular postmodern opinion, truth by its very definition cannot be one thing for me and another for you. Truth is exclusive and leaves no wriggle room for subjective individualism.

As Christians seeking maturity in our quest for knowledge and understanding – solid food beyond the milk of our early Christian life – engaging with reason-based arguments will only serve to deepen the reasonableness of our faith. We have nothing to fear in regard to losing our faith through such discussions, as the faith and truth we have received has been, and continues to be, revealed to us by the spirit of God himself.

'And I will ask the Father, and he will give you another advocate to help you and be with you forever – the Spirit of truth. The world cannot accept him, because it neither sees him nor knows him. But you know him, for he lives with you and will be in you' (Jn 14:16–17).

For like Paul, the truth of the gospel that we preach is not something we have made up.

'I did not receive it from any man, nor was I taught it; rather, I received it by revelation from Jesus Christ' (Gal 1:12).

The evidence we present and the reasons we use in our arguments for truth will have no standing with those who have not had their hearts and minds illuminated by Christ, particularly for those who adamantly reject Christ, holding firmly to their self-constructed versions of truth.

So then, in a world of preformed ideas, are our efforts in providing a reason for our faith of any use? With Christ involved, it's a resounding *yes!* – because those who are blind can indeed be set free to see, and maybe, just maybe, our reasoned arguments will take part in the process.

Professor Henry Van Til once proposed that faith, being a gift from God through the regenerating work of the Holy Spirit, acts as a wedge that divides humanity.[3] Van Til makes an

---

3 Henry R. Van Til, *The Calvinistic Concept of Culture*, Baker Academic, Grand Rapids MI, 1972, p. 179.

important point in that humanity is (and will continue to be) divided until the last day, whereupon the shroud will finally be lifted and truth will be seen in all its glory. On that great day, all debates on reason and truth will be eternally put to rest.

Until that day arrives, however, as long as we have a mind to learn and a mouth to speak, we are called to give a reason for what we believe.

But in your hearts revere Christ as Lord. Always be prepared to give an answer to everyone who asks you to give the reason for the hope that you have. But do this with gentleness and respect (1 Pet 3:15).

Apologetics beyond Mount Stupid

In Christian circles, the art of apologetics – providing a reasonable defence for the Christian faith – is becoming increasingly prominent and important, particularly as social media simplifies the process of conversation on a global scale. How can we become more effective in the area of Christian apologetics then?

I believe a good starting point can be found in the following words of Forrest Gump: 'Stupid is as stupid does'.[4]

Now, stay with me here. Forrest makes a good point. Stupidity is not defined by one's intellect but rather by one's actions. In the realm of apologetics, to be arrogant is to appear stupid. We need to keep in mind that we are called to reflect Christ in our conversations, and Christ was gentle and humble in heart.

So how do we avoid appearing stupid when it comes to our ability to argue for our faith? Firstly, we might learn from a simple but interesting study conducted in 1999 by Dunning and Kruger, which became known as the 'Dunning-Kruger Effect'.[5]

---

4 Quoted from the film *Forrest Gump*, Paramount Pictures, A Steve Tisch/ Wendy Finerman Production, A Robert Zemeckis Film, 1994.
5 For more information on the 'Dunning-Kruger Effect' see: https:// en.wikipedia.org/wiki/Dunning–Kruger_effect

This study demonstrated a psychological phenomenon in which individuals foolishly believe they have enough knowledge about a subject to be vocal about it, despite not having obtained enough knowledge around the subject to engage in discussions that reflect any real wisdom on their behalf.

Perhaps the more well-known, less scientific version of the Dunning-Kruger Effect is referred to as climbing Mount Stupid. Until a person reaches the peak of Mount Stupid, they will continue in their delusion of expertise until finally they reach the point where they come to terms with their own ignorance. At this point they become willing to slide to the bottom of the uncomfortable slope where they can resume a realistic building of knowledge, this time in a state of humility.

For the Christian apologist, the quicker one can ascend Mount Stupid, reaching the point of humbly acknowledging areas of personal ignorance, the better. Let's just get it out of the way! There's no point pretending we can advise professors on how they are wrong about their own areas of expertise just because we've read an article or two on the subject. The advantage the Christian has, however, is that Christ demands humility from us from the beginning; he asks that we make our descent before him as we come to a child-like dependence on him from the moment we are called.

And he said: 'Truly I tell you, unless you change and become like little children, you will never enter the kingdom of heaven' (Mt 18:3).

Having contemplated the need to avoid being stuck on the ignorant side of Mount Stupid, we need to consider what the apologist needs to immerse themselves in so as to provide reasonable arguments for their faith. Strangely, I believe we can learn here from an unlikely teacher: the fighter. If you've ever had a conversation with an experienced fighter, one with extensive experience in the ring, they will tell you that no training measures up to real combat. Take for instance the words of Mike

Tyson: 'Everyone has a plan – until they get punched in the face'.[6] In other words, having conversations and healthy debates with people regarding the reasonableness of the Christian faith will swiftly deliver blows to areas of our personal ignorance, helping to point us to where our knowledge needs to grow. Of course, we can also learn from those who have many years of experience answering the deepest of questions and responding with reason to the unreasonable. Respected apologists such as Alister McGrath and John Lennox are prime examples.

An excellent starting point in the apologist's journey would be to consider: 'Does Christianity and its understanding of God stand tall when subjected to questions of reason?'

Throughout history, there have been several well-reasoned arguments for the existence of God. Cosmological arguments that revolve around the need for an intelligent Creator, the mind and energy behind the Big Bang and the birth of the universe, have been discussed extensively. Moral arguments have been put forward suggesting that our sense of right and wrong must originate from an ultimate source of morality: God. It is important to keep in mind, though, that well-reasoned arguments in these areas remain unable to provide proof beyond any doubt for the existence of the Christian God. We must, as apologists, come to terms with the fact that many answers can only be left to faith, whether others accept this or not.

> *This is what we speak, not in words taught us by human wisdom but in words taught by the Spirit, explaining spiritual realities with Spirit-taught words. The person without the Spirit does not accept the things that come from the Spirit of God but considers them foolishness, and cannot understand them because they are discerned only through the Spirit (1 Cor 2:13–14).*

The question of whether Christianity can stand tall in the

---

6 These words are Mike Tyson's response to a question from a reporter in the lead-up to his fight against Evander Holyfield.

face of reason will never be answered with a resounding 'Yes!' For if reason alone could explain the reality of God, then faith would become obsolete. The good news for the Christian is that by the ongoing, transforming work of the Holy Spirit, we are able to understand the reasonableness of our faith.

And so, as Christian apologists, we would do well to accept that the God given gift of faith provides us with the only means of truly comprehending God's truth about his existence, his nature and his revelation and plan for his people. We are called, therefore, to use our intellect in a way that is humbly and spiritually driven, prayerfully acknowledging that any effective apologetics on our behalf is completely dependent on God and his purposes. This is apologetics beyond Mount Stupid.

Reasons of the heart

If you scroll through the vast web of apologetics articles and quotes floating around in cyberspace, you'll see that there exists a mountain of well-reasoned arguments focusing on the scientific and philosophical support for the validity of the Christian faith. It's easy to become caught up in these fascinating, deep contemplations, as I have done, dedicating time to writing related arguments from a personal perspective.

I wonder, however, whether Christian apologists focus too much energy on arguments that reside in the arena of logic and reason, rather than in the realm of human needs and grace. Are we unwittingly avoiding addressing the issues that deeply affect us all? Do we sacrifice the heart for the head?

But really, we should ask, how can those of us tasked with giving a reason for our faith *not* share the peace that surpasses all understanding? When it comes to topics such as suffering and death, topics of unavoidable human struggle, how can we *not* take the opportunity to present a case for a merciful, loving God?

And the peace of God, which transcends all understanding,

will guard your hearts and your minds in Christ Jesus (Phil 4:7).

Surely, if we are to be effective apologists for the Christian faith, we are to share the peace of God with those whose paths we cross each day. We cannot rely solely on elaborate, logically formed arguments to convince others of the truth about what God has achieved through Christ. We are called to do more than that. Christians must become a place in which the word is alive through the transforming work of the Holy Spirit. This means living in a way that reflects God's grace and points people to his truth and the peace that it brings. These are matters in which the heart cannot be ignored.

Perhaps this is why French mathematician and philosopher Blaise Pascal came to believe that faith in God transcends reason as it flows from the heart – and the heart has its reasons, which reason knows nothing about.[7]

It's worth stopping to reflect on what it means for something to flow from the heart. Perhaps Pascal's idea speaks to us because deep down we all struggle to align all of logic and reason with our human emotions. We are, after all, more closely related to Captain Kirk than to Spock.[8] While we might know something to be true within our minds, our hearts can seem to whisper alternative words of wisdom into our being, often blurring the lines around the choices we must make.

When we are faced with seemingly unbearable moral dilemmas, the kind that have us making difficult decisions, perhaps even situations involving life or death outcomes, how will we come to our conclusions? I can only imagine the unbearable tension that exists in the hearts and minds of political leaders as they make decisions affecting the lives of

---

7 Chapman, *Case for Christianity*, p. 169.
8 For the uninitiated, Captain Kirk and Spock are contrasting characters from the Star Trek films and television series. Captain Kirk embraced his humanity and often followed his emotions when making decisions. Spock, on the other hand, was only half human. It was his logic-driven, Vulcan half that influenced most of his thinking.

millions of people. While few of us are called to such positions of great power and leadership, we still need to consider how we will justify our decisions as followers of Christ in a world that sees his wisdom as foolishness.

Balancing human logic and emotion can certainly pull us in different directions, but as Christians we are called to seek the counsel of Christ, whose unchanging heart and mind provide us with the only reliable moral compass. While our natural tendencies may cause us to lose our bearings, the wisdom of Christ remains our true north.

The question is, as we look to Christ, whom will we find?

And the Word was God

My father once told me a story of an elderly lady who attended his church for many years, only to abandon her faith after hearing a sermon that conflicted with her long-held belief that Jesus Christ was in fact an Englishman. While this may seem ridiculous, it does raise an important question. 'How is it that any person within a church community can come to hold beliefs that lie so far from the truth revealed in God's word?'

Isn't this the same problem that enables agenda-driven television networks such as the ABC to host guests on Q&A panels who claim to represent mainstream Christianity while simultaneously rejecting the resurrection of Christ?

To truly understand how this happens, I believe we need to travel all the way back to the beginning, to where the heart of humanity first turned from its Creator. Since that dark day, people have continued in their thirst for equality with God, to know his thoughts, to even control his thoughts, all in the name of 'the self'. It seems we are not, nor have we ever been, exclusively satisfied with the Logos, the Word of God, revealed to us in Christ. Instead, we seek to comprehend the incomprehensible, the hidden God, a God that in the end is often created in our own image according to human reason.

This is how even those who attend Christian churches come to adopt twisted, alternative versions of God's truth. Left to our own devices, a Jewish rabbi can even lose his historical roots and somehow become an Englishman.

Perhaps this is why John Calvin suggests, 'The human heart has so many recesses for vanity, so many lurking places for falsehood, is so shrouded by fraud and hypocrisy that it often deceives itself'.[9]

> *Above all else, guard your heart, for everything you do flows from it. Keep your mouth free from perversity; keep corrupt talk far from your lips. Let your eyes look straight ahead, fix your gaze directly before you. Give careful thought to the paths for your feet and be steadfast in all your ways. Do not turn to the right or the left; keep your foot from evil (Prov 4:23–27).*

Without eyes focused firmly on Christ, Christians are not exempt from this self-deceit.

Is it not true that even those who are being transformed to be more Christ-like, contrary to their ultimate longings to live in communion with God, still fall short of the perfection of Christ? Are they not at war with their own tendencies to manipulate God for their own purposes? Surely, we all at times need to be dragged back into Job's quivering boots, to be confronted once again by the truth about our place before God as mere mortals.

> *'Who is this that obscures my plans with words without knowledge? Brace yourself like a man; I will question you, and you will answer me … Will the one who contends with the Almighty correct him? Let him who accuses God answer him' (Job 38:2–3 and 40:2).*

What then is the answer to the ongoing conflict within the hearts and minds of Christians and between those within the church? Surely our interpretation of Scripture and the

---

9 John Calvin, *The Institutes of the Christian Religion*, Christian Ethereal Library, Grand Rapids MI, 1947. (Public Domain)

authority we assign to it correlates with the opinions we form and the decisions we make, both on a personal and church community level?

To live a Christian life is to follow Christ, and walking in his light depends on our ability to recognise and listen to his voice. Perhaps this is why Jesus challenges us with these words right before his parable about building our lives on the rock:

'Why do you call me, "Lord, Lord," and do not do what I say?' *(Lk 6:46).*

These words should sink deep into the conscience of anyone seeking to truly follow Christ. Wisdom is not formed by the one who is blown around by the influences of alternative truths but rather in submitting to the Logos – God's wisdom revealed in Christ. As Martin Luther wrote, 'the Power of Scripture is this: it will not be altered by the one who studies it; instead it transforms the one who loves it'.[10]

It's once we cease to test doctrines and interpret Scripture with Scripture that the foundations upon which we stand soon crumble, leaving us with a mishmash of subjective opinions formed by self-serving human beings.

Without being anchored to the rock of God revealed through Christ, the Church and its' people become increasingly indistinguishable from the world around them. The light that once shone brightly becomes hidden under the veil of tolerance for alternative truths and current agendas trending in society.

What we desire as Christians should align with what God wants. This is the path to the narrow gate through which we enter his pastures and his rest. Jesus words are very clear:

'If you hold to my teaching, you are really my disciples. Then you will know the truth, and the truth will set you free' (Jn 8:31–32).

We are called to submit with childlike humility to what has been revealed to us in God's word. He knows what leads us

---

10 Oswald Bayer, *Martin Luther's Theology: A Contemporary Application*, Eerdmans, Grand Rapids MI, 2008, p. 71.

to life, because he *is* life, having spoken all of life into being, breathing breath into each one of us. And so, as we seek to interpret the complex world in which we live, let it be done through the wisdom of Christ. When we seek illumination to interpret his word, let our interpretations be tested with his inspired Scripture. When anybody makes a claim on God's behalf, let the claim be analysed under the exposing light of Christ.

Is it clear then to whom you belong? Is there any doubt in the eyes of those in your life as to the source of your faith, hope and truth?

In the words of Jesus not long before his execution, *'Not my will, but yours be done' (Lk 22:42).*

The contentious cross

As Christians, there will always be one thing that uniquely defines us from all other claims to truth: the cross of Christ. Throughout history, nothing has been the cause of more contention and division than the cross. As we engage in truth debates with those who deny Christ, this remains an unavoidable stumbling block.

But why?

I believe the divisive nature of the message of the cross stems from the strong contrast between the wisdom of Christ and the wisdom of the world, and this comes to a head in the cross of Christ.

Our personal view on the cross will to a large extent depend on our view of truth, especially the truth about ourselves in relation to sin and our need for salvation. While it is a fundamental belief in Christian circles that we have inherited a sinful nature from our ancestor Adam, this is by no means a universal, worldly understanding of the human condition.

One classic example is the Hindu perspective on sin and salvation. In 1983, a lecture was held in the first Parliament of Religions in Chicago where Swami Vivekananda, a Hindu reformer, said, 'The Hindu refuses to call you sinners. Ye are the children of God; the sharers of immortal bliss, holy and perfect beings. Ye divinities on earth, sinners? It is a sin to call a man a sinner. It is a standing libel on human nature.'[11]

For those who follow a teaching that defines humanity as anything other than innately sinful and needing salvation from a source beyond ourselves, the cross of Christ will surely seem foolishness – even offensive.

For the Jews of Jesus' day, to be crucified in the humiliating and torturous way as had been perfected by the Roman executioners was far removed from their idea of messianic victory. To be crucified was to be cursed (Deut 21:22–23), so surely this was not the destiny of their long-awaited Messiah – not the culmination of God's wisdom. According to their Scriptures, however, the crucifixion was exactly what had been foretold by the prophet Isaiah. Take this small section of his prophetic words:

> *But he was pierced for our transgressions, he was crushed for our iniquities; the punishment that brought us peace was on him, and by his wounds we are healed. We all, like sheep, have gone astray, each of us has turned to our own way; and the Lord has laid on him the iniquity of us all (Isa 53:5–6).*

It seems that ever since people attempted to assume God's place as Lord, they have refused to believe the truth, exchanging it for a lie. It's not surprising, then, that when many seek a form of spirituality, they are drawn to teachings that affirm their personal goodness and individualistic right to divinity.

It is for this reason that Christians place the cross of Christ at the centre of their lives; it is God's ultimate wisdom. To deny the resurrection and what Christ achieved on the cross is to deny Christ himself. If the resurrection is a lie, then Paul, a great leader in the early church would have to have

---

11 John Stott, *Evangelical Truth*, Inter-Varsity, Nottingham, 2003, p. 88.

been a false teacher. The Christian hope he spoke of, that of being resurrected in Christ, would be worthless. But as any respectable historian would have to concede, for Paul to lie in this way just doesn't add up. Why would a highly respected and well-positioned Christian-hating Roman citizen suddenly give up everything and devote his entire life to serving and suffering for the one he was so adamant on destroying? There really is only one explanation. He came to know the risen Christ. For him, Christ's cross is the focal point of Christian faith, just as it was central to the mind of Jesus himself. The reality of Paul's conversion can be clearly seen in his new-found perspective on the cross.

May I never boast except in the cross of our Lord Jesus Christ, through which the world has been crucified to me, and I to the world (Gal 6:14).

Paul was well aware of the divisiveness the cross brings to a world of people who reject Christ.

Jews demand signs and Greeks look for wisdom, but we preach Christ crucified; a stumbling block to Jews and foolishness to Gentiles, but to those whom God has called, both Jews and Greeks, Christ the power of God and the wisdom of God (1 Cor 1:22–24).

Effectively reflecting Christ back into the world, providing apologetics beyond reason, requires us to view the cross in the same way, always returning to it as we proclaim God's truth to the world. After all, it's the only real hope we have.

But Christ has indeed been raised from the dead, the firstfruits of those who have fallen asleep. For since death came through a man, the resurrection of the dead comes also through a man. For as in Adam all die, so in Christ all will be made alive (1 Cor 15:20–22).

4. True Love

> The beautiful simplicity of our faith is that it distils down to the exact same bottom line for both the brilliant theologian and the five-year-old child: love God and love each other – period.[1] (Richard Stearns)

I once attended a memorial service for a well-loved primary school teacher who had died, and I was overwhelmed by the intimate affect that one person could have on the lives of many others. Upon reflection, this remarkable woman's legacy was so profound because her life, once unfolded and relived through those closest to her, embodied the essence of Stearn's statement. It was said of her that while some people collect all manner of things, she collected people – people who responded to the genuine love shown for both God and others. To attend such a celebration of life is to buy a ticket to ride a rollercoaster of emotion, one that carries you from sorrow, to joy, to pure inspiration.

Several years ago, singer-songwriter Stevie Nicks wrote a song called *Landslide*,[2] in which she questioned the idea of love and our ability to cope with the changing seasons of our lives.

Here, in reflections such as these, we find a question that no person can avoid. Can any of us handle the seasons of our lives? While there are many different ways of seeking to sail through changing ocean tides, few would disagree that 'love' must be part of the answer. But what is love? Or more importantly, what is *real* love?

What's God got to do with it?

---

1 Richard Stearns, 'Be an Ambassador of God's Love', 2014. https://www.faithgateway.com/be-an-ambassador-of-love/#.XG4J_vZuI2w
2 Stevie Nicks, *Landslide*, (Reprise, 1975). Recorded by the band Fleetwood Mac and produced by Keith Olson.

Where can I go from your spirit? Where can I flee from your presence? If I go up to the heavens, you are there. If I make my bed in the depths, you are there. If I rise on the wings of the dawn, if I settle on the far side of the sea, even there your hand will guide me, your right hand will hold me fast (Ps 139:7–10).

It's no secret that Christians hold firm to the belief that God is love. As it says in 1 John, *'Whoever does not love does not know God, because God is love' (1 Jn 4:8).*

But how does this translate in the minds of those drowning in the depths of tragedy?

The heartfelt cries of human loss echo ceaselessly through time, asking, 'Where is God in the natural disaster? Where is God in the midst of genocide? Where is God when disease mercilessly attacks its undeserving victims?'

'The Lord giveth and the Lord taketh away.' This throwaway line has become somewhat clichéd in today's general conversation, but I suspect its origins are more closely tied to a place of great suffering. Deep down, it probably speaks to some of our greatest fears. As we naturally come to deeply love the people and things of this life, doesn't the potential of losing them sometimes become more emotionally crippling than even the fear of death itself?

And then comes the next question. Does God really care?

When things go wrong – and they always will at some point in our lives – we often seek to blame someone or something for the injustice that has taken place. The ultimate blame, however, is usually directed at God himself. This seems a perfectly natural human response. If you've just watched a dearly loved family member wither away in the merciless hands of cancer while an all-powerful, all-knowing God seems to ignore your deepest cries for help, hearing from Christians that everything is part of a divine tapestry weaved in love can be a bitter pill to swallow.

Surely if God were a God of love, he would end our suffering and bring about peace and prosperity for us all. How can a God who really cares appear so withdrawn from the cries of his creation?

'I cry out to you, O God, but you do not answer; I stand up, but you merely look at me' (Job 30:20).

These are human questions, and like Job, who suffered perhaps more than any other, we need to hear God's answers, even when they stand far apart from the opinions of the world. We need to draw closer to the heart of God.

A Father's love

It may be difficult for us to conceive of this truth, but God's ability to relate to his people and the depth of his love are infinitely greater than we can ever comprehend. He has, however, placed in our possession powerful, historical and scriptural accounts of his love that, through the work of his Spirit, can take us to a place of understanding, a place where our heart strings may become entwined with his, if even only for a moment. It is in such moments that we come to grasp just a little of the sacrifice he has made for us.

A powerful lesson can be learned about the depth of God's love for us when we consider the story of Abraham and his beloved son Isaac. For a parent, the thought of losing a child – and for some, the experience of losing a child – is as devastating a blow as life can deliver. So, when Abraham is asked by God to sacrifice his precious son, we can come to understand the mental torment this would have brought about.

Why then did God, knowing the pain that his request would cause Abraham, continue to test his faith in this way? Is it that faith in God's promises is ultimately strengthened in the midst of pain and suffering, when all we have is the ability to fall helplessly into the saving grace of our Heavenly Father?

By faith Abraham, when God tested him, offered Isaac as a sacrifice. He who had embraced the promises was about to sacrifice his one and only son, even though God had said to him, 'It is through Isaac that your offspring will be reckoned.' Abraham reasoned that God could even raise the dead, and so in a manner of speaking, he did receive Isaac back from death (Heb 11:17–19).

Interestingly, it's at the point when we come to empathise with Abraham in the sacrifice he was willing to make for God that we can truly understand a little of the depth of love God has for his people, including us. When all seemed lost for Isaac, and his final heart beat seemed fast approaching, God intervened.

'Do not lay a hand on the boy,' he said. 'Do not do anything to him. Now I know that you fear God, because you have not withheld from me your son, your only son' (Gen 22:12).

God provided not only a ram in place of Isaac but also his one and only Son with whom he is well pleased. Surely as we contemplate this, we can start to comprehend the true sacrifice made by him – an act of love so profound that even while our hearts were far from him, he was crucified for our sin.

Yet it was the Lord's will to crush him and to cause him to suffer, and though the Lord makes his life an offering for sin, he will see his offspring and prolong his days, and the will of the Lord will prosper in his hand (Isa 53:10).

And so it is that God shows love for his people: the Father has given the Son with whom he is well pleased, the Son has given his life for the ransom of many, and the Holy Spirit has been given so that we may grow in faith through the life-changing grace offered to us.

A God of intimacy

The truth is that God is far from being removed from the lives of his people. He knows all about suffering, because he knows all about relationship. After all, the three persons of the Trinity have been living in a perfect love relationship eternally. While many aspects of God will remain incomprehensible to us, one thing is clear: God is a God of love, relating to himself in perfect love. He therefore suffered greatly when the Son was cruelly sacrificed under the weight of humanity's sin.

While pain, suffering and loss will continue to rear their ugly heads throughout our lives, it can bring us comfort to know that, when we need a God who is bigger than ourselves and who can relate to the anguish that so often accompanies loss and grief, our God understands and loves us. Not only does he want what's best for us, but he's already taken care of it. As Jesus said on the cross, 'It is finished'.

> *God's dwelling place is now among the people, and he will dwell with them. They will be his people, and God himself will be with them and be their God. He will wipe every tear from their eyes. There will be no more death or mourning or crying or pain, for the old order of things has passed away (Rev 21:3–4).*

God's love reflectors

What we have discovered is that it's the way in which we interpret the phrase 'God is love' that becomes important to how it impacts our life. Our understanding of God as love will be shaped by our understanding of God in relation to both himself and his creation. It is only in the relationship expressed in the Trinity that we can fully understand love, as this is the source of all eternal love.

'Love is not eternal because the poet may ever so beautifully say so, but rather because God is eternal and says so. Each person in the Godhead eternally loves the other persons. God eternally loves God and his neighbour as himself.'[3]

To the Christian, it is clear that to understand love, and

---

[3] McKinlay, *Song of Creation*, p. 19.

indeed to be truly loving, we must be in Christ, whose love exists eternally in the perfect loving relationship of the Trinity. The Triune God can identify with our human stories because he has firsthand experience with the emotions tied to our experiences of love. We see this time and again as we experience God as he has been revealed to us in the life of Christ.

'Anyone who has seen me has seen the Father' (Jn 14:9).

As we come to see love in light of God's true nature, we come to a deeper appreciation of how great a sacrifice Christ made on our behalf as he took upon himself the sins of the whole world. Christ the Son, eternally existing in perfect love with the Father, being separated from him as he took upon himself the curse rightfully owned by humanity, is an act of love we will never fully comprehend.

While there is mystery surrounding the events of the cross, just as there is mystery as to why people have love for one another at all, what was achieved through Christ on the cross helps us make sense of our own love.

'We love because he [Christ] first loved us' (1 Jn 4:19).

When it comes to 'love' there is much to be said and much that has been said. I wonder if the band, 'The Beatles', when they bombarded the airwaves with, 'All you need is love', had any idea of the truth that lay behind these words. While these words ring true in many ears, their power becomes real only when they acknowledge that 'God is love'. All we need is God and the perfect love that can only be found in the relationship of the Trinity. In the Father's deep love for the Son, we who belong to Christ have been given to him as a loving gift from the Father.

Thank God for the people in our lives who truly bear his image by reflecting his love in their lives. These are the people whose theology shines as light in the darkness through their simple acts of loving God and loving others.

People who need people

I will never forget the day I received a phone call informing me that my sponsor child, Samuel Mtembo, whom I'd been supporting for a number of years, had suddenly died of an unexplained medical condition. On this day, I remembered hearing a preacher suggest that we will never look into the eyes of anyone who doesn't matter to God. I never did get the opportunity to look into the eyes of my sponsor child, but I know for sure that he mattered to God, and therefore he mattered to me. Having received correspondence from his family for many years, I know that I mattered to him also. These types of relationships give us reason to ask questions about how we should see others in a world that often promotes seeing only the person in the mirror.

Christianity, though embedded in the truth, loses its power when it becomes a mere academic exercise, devoid of actions that suggest that people really matter. Christianity cannot become aligned with an individualistic culture focused on serving the self. Truth that is not expressed through love will always appear cold and often repulsive.

Let us not forget what Jesus taught about how we should see others.

'A new command I give you: Love one another. As I have loved you, so you must love one another. By this everyone will know that you are my disciples, if you love one another' (Jn 13:34–35).

These words of Christ are not unfamiliar to many of us, but they raise the question, 'Why is it that we find it so difficult to genuinely and unconditionally love others?' After all, we all know on a deep, personal level that we need to be loved. We are all people who need people.

For those of us who live in the West, it has become increasingly easy to form and express opinions and ideas about people we don't really know or understand, particularly in the digital world. It's not a surprise that living lives hidden behind screens and devices, with the concomitant absence of body language and face-to-face human emotion, leads to so much relational breakdown. However, the moment we come face to face with real people in real places, preconceived thoughts and biases often melt away. Human relationships can instead be defined in the context of an emotional reality.

Peter Vardy, in his book *Being Human*, gives us some insight into why we consistently fail to genuinely love others by taking us to the roots of the Western world's increasingly perceived lack of meaning. He suggests:

'Seeing human beings as a biological accident without meaning or purpose has led to many of the difficulties at the heart of modern society. This has been accompanied by an ethical impotence because no intellectual framework seems to exist to challenge this meaninglessness.'[4]

Martin Luther understood this problem well and expressed it in the context of the Christian faith, particularly in response to the writings of Paul in 1 Corinthians 9:19. Luther writes:

'A Christian is a free lord over all things and is subject to no one. A Christian is a ready servant of all things and is subject to everyone.'[5]

It is because of the freedom we have gained through the perfect love of what God has accomplished through Christ, and the knowledge revealed to us about who we are as purpose-built human beings, that we are able to live for others in Christ's name.

> *We love because he first loved us. Whoever claims to love God yet hates a brother or sister is a liar. For whoever does not love their brother and sister, whom they have seen, cannot love God, whom they have not seen. And he has given us this command: anyone who loves God must also love their brother and sister (1 Jn 4:19–21).*

---

4 Peter Vardy, *Being Human*, p. 193.
5 Bayer, *Martin Luther's Theology*, p. 289.

We can only conclude that the human race consists of 'people who need people'. We must then ask ourselves if we will become the people who love other people. Will we love others through our freedom in Christ and with the help of his Holy Spirit?

Peace beyond the tribe

Do we really, deep down, desire peace for and with everyone we cross paths with? Or is our desire for peace more selective and confined to those who are like us – a love saved for those whose image reflects at least a little of ourselves or the people we seek to be?

The problem with humanity is that we behave like human beings, subconsciously under the influence of a biological condition that has us dancing to our DNA. We constantly strive for survival and acceptance within the human pack, seeking to fit in using whatever means necessary until we establish so called immortality through the passing on of our genes.

Tribalism – the group mentality – seems inescapable to members of a species who need to be accepted, to fit in. Tribalism is all around us, and none of us is exempt. From the school yard to politics, religion to race, sporting clubs to fashion, the boundaries of our worlds overlap, separate and collide.

A few decades ago, in my home town of Melbourne, Australia, tribalism ran strong through the veins of suburbanites as football teams formed lines of separation that were not to be crossed. Typically, your postcode dictated the football team you were to support with all of your heart, mind, soul and strength – a tribe that defined a large proportion of your identity as a Melbournian. Stories of young men wandering into the territory of rival teams ended in bloody brawls, participants using everything down to the pickets from fences to defend the pride and territory of their tribe. But obviously this type of madness is not exclusive. Temporary or otherwise, insanity often flows from the heart of tribalism.

With the mentality of tribalism based on such simple things as football teams, yet causing emotionally driven acts of hate and violence, what hope do we have for peace in a world where the 'them and us' extends to so many different contexts? While hate is never acceptable, it is often the result of complex, deep-seated and historical tensions between the 'them and us'.

A conundrum seems to exist within the human race; there's a tension between the peace we desire and the group mentalities that drive a dualistic wedge between us as members of the tribe known as 'humanity'.

Is there a solution to this age-old problem, or will we simply have to settle for the well-meaning platitudes of Miss Universe contestants?

It seems in our search for a pathway to world peace that many of us, at least in the Western world, identify with John Lennon's *Imagine*.[6] But before hitching a ride on this bandwagon, it just might be worth contemplating what the lyrics to this song suggest. Do we really want to imagine heaven to be non-existent, crushing the hope of a better world beyond the now and the future that we have a promised part in? Do we really want to imagine the death of religion and therefore God, leaving us without significance and meaning beyond random chance?

While this song may serve as an emotional anthem for humanists, the existence of one who stretches far beyond the limits of our finite comprehension is a reality linked to a deeper hope, far greater than humanity alone can ever offer.

It may not align with popular Western opinion, but the solution to peace in a tribalistic, dualistic world can only be found in the Scriptures. Imagine that!

We need to come to the realisation that although we identify with many different tribes, we all belong to the human tribe.

---

6 Lennon, John, *Imagine*, Apple, 1971.

Understanding this from a biblical perspective can have far-reaching implications; life can be seen through God's eyes, so to speak.

So God created mankind in his own image; in the image of God he created him; male and female he created them (Gen 1:27).

Peace pleads for us to open our eyes to the realisation that all people matter to God. You will never look into the eyes of another human being who does not matter to God. This reality alone should see the divisive walls of the 'them and us' crumbling as we comprehend the intended diversity of humanity and the fact that we are all included in a non-random sacred creation, purpose built to live in harmony with both God and each other.

To take this concept to an even deeper level, we must look to Christ, the Messiah, king of those who have faith.

He was given authority, glory and sovereign power; all nations and peoples of every language worshipped him. His dominion is an everlasting dominion that will not pass away, and his kingdom is one that will never be destroyed (Dan 7:14).

To follow Christ is to be a part of something far greater than any tribe. We are invited to be members of a kingdom, ruled by the king appointed by the Ancient of Days from the beginning, a king also known as the Prince of Peace. Surely the path to peace lies in following this king, serving him through an unwavering allegiance to his kingship. Our hope for peace calls out for us to follow in the dust of Rabbi Jesus so that we may learn his ways.

History can be a powerful teacher, and we should be able to learn from our terrible, bloody past. Yet we don't seem to be making much progress. While dualistic natures continue to divide societies, waging all kinds of wars between those created in God's image, the unworn path to peace starts with the words of our King:

'"*Love the Lord your God with all your heart and with all your soul and with all your mind." This is the first and greatest commandment. And the second is like it: "Love your neighbour as yourself." All the Law and the Prophets hang on these two commandments*' (Mt 22:37–40).

'*Blessed are the merciful, for they will be shown mercy. Blessed are the pure in heart, for they will see God. Blessed are the peacemakers, for they will be called children of God*' (Mt 5:7–9).

5. Beyond the Fish Sticker

Dr Nakashima Atsumi, in his preface to *True Path of the Ninja*, suggests that to live with spiritual richness within modern society, among the ever-widening gap between the rich and the poor, you need to change your sense of value and be confident in yourself.[1] I find it interesting that even in the pages of ancient Japanese philosophies, the promotion of 'the self' still takes centre stage. Who could ever forget the famous line from Mohammad Ali's lips, 'I am the greatest! I'm the greatest thing that ever lived'. Ali, while voicing these words, highlights just how far the heart of humanity has strayed from the heart of Christ.

If we really seek truth as it exists in Christian Scripture – that is, to desire the message of Christ and what he asks of us – we will find a message so profound and so challenging that it will tear us away, if we allow it, from the very fabric of worldly wisdom. It will lead us into a truth that exists as a polar opposite to the messages that have been imbedded in our consciousness and cultural DNA since the fall of humankind. This truth, however, comes with a price attached. Christianity involves far more than placing a fish sticker on your car.

The cost

Several years ago, while studying at La Trobe University in Melbourne, Australia, I came across a guy who was changed by the gospel message. He had come to university with plans to complete a degree in commerce before entering the world of finance, a high-powered corporate arena that would set him up well by worldly standards. The challenge for him came when

---

1 Antony Cummins and Yoshie Minami, *True Path of the Ninja*, Turtle, North Clarendon VT, 2017. See preface by Dr Nakashima Atsumi.

the gospel message transformed his goals into those of Christ. This didn't go down very smoothly with his atheistic father, who simply saw his son throwing his future down the toilet. But this story isn't unique and shouldn't come as a surprise. Jesus never inferred that he came to make our lives easy or filled with wealth and pleasure. Consider his words:

> 'Do not suppose that I have come to bring peace to the earth. I did not come to bring peace, but a sword. For I have come to turn a man against his father, a daughter against her mother, a daughter-in-law against her mother-in-law – a man's enemies will be members of his own household' (Mt 10:34–36).

These are hardly comforting words. Yet they are words that ring true, especially for those who have become isolated and banished from places such as Jewish, Hindu and Islamic households for the sake of Christ.

Before he died, Islamic-turned-Christian writer Nabeel Qureshi shared in his book about a young woman from Saudi Arabia who truly understood what it means to sacrifice one's life in order to save it.[2] A member of Islamic group *Al-Hasba* assassinated his sister for converting from Islam to following Christ; he killed her by burning her and cutting out her tongue. Why would a young girl in her prime lay down her life in such a way? She knew that by losing her life for Christ she was really gaining it.

The struggle for survival is certainly in our DNA. The idea of choosing to die to ourselves for the sake of gaining life through Christ is counterintuitive. It goes against the grain of everything we feel. It is far removed from our role in the 'survival of the fittest'. It is for this reason that the goals of psychology and theology often don't see eye to eye.

Psychology can, however, give us some interesting insights into human behaviour. It has been recognised that people show an overt desire for conformity and to be part of a group.

---

2 N. Qureshi, *No God but One*, Zondervan, Grand Rapids MI, 2016, pp. 294–5.

It's natural for us to want to conform to the world's way of thinking in order to avoid exclusion or suffer a demotion of self-worth through popular opinion. After all, who wants to be caught wearing a skinny tie in a fat tie year?

In 1954, psychologist Maslow proposed a theory for human motivation, which he represented using a pyramid consisting of multiple layers. This 'pyramid of needs' was used to show the hierarchy of needs that must be met to achieve self-actualisation. Maslow suggested that these needs provide the motivation for all human endeavour. At the bottom of the pyramid are the most fundamental physical needs (physiological needs, safety and security, love and belonging, self-esteem) and at the apex lies self-actualisation, the ultimate universal goal of the human being.[3] Once again, we come to a way of thinking that suggests the serving of the self as the ultimate goal.

An interesting question for Christians to ask then would be, 'What does it mean to live in the world but not of the world, and how does this relate to taking up my cross?'

In *Mere Christianity*, C.S. Lewis writes:

> Christ says, 'Give me all. I don't want so much of your time and so much of your money and so much of your work: I want you. I have not come to torment your natural self, but to kill it. No half measures are any good. I don't want to cut off a branch here and a branch there. I want to have the whole tree down. I don't want to drill the tooth, or crown it, or stop it, but to have it out.'[4]

Lewis has a brilliant way of illustrating things, and his writings point clearly to a very challenging part of what Jesus asks of us all: to lay down our life, only to take it up again in him.

> *'Whoever wants to be my disciple must deny themselves and take up their cross daily and follow me. For whoever wants to save their life will lose it, but whoever loses their life for me*

3 Rooney, *Story of Psychology*, pp. 178–9.
4 C.S. Lewis, *Complete C.S. Lewis*, p. 104.

will save it. What good is it for someone to gain the whole world, and yet lose or forfeit their very self?' (Lk 9:23–25)

To die to oneself for the sake of following Christ is a challenge to say the least. It requires a humility that is very rare in this world and goes against everything that the world equates with success. No doubt this is why Jesus himself recognised that the task is impossible as he spoke to a rich young ruler seeking eternal life. This upright man was unable to deny himself of his wealth in order to gain eternal life. Consider Jesus' words:

'Again I tell you, it is easier for a camel to go through the eye of a needle than for someone who is rich to enter the Kingdom of God.'

Jesus doesn't leave us without hope, however. He adds the words:

'With man this is impossible, but with God all things are possible' (Mt 19:24, 26).

While it's true that Jesus asks the impossible from us, it *is* possible to be transformed as the Holy Spirit works within our hearts and minds, helping us to develop the childlike humility needed to surrender to Christ. It is here, in the place of true surrender, that we are finally set free to live as the person we have been created to be.

A risk worth the gain

When it comes to Christianity, there's no escaping the effects of subjecting your life to the truth of Christ as revealed in Scripture. If both the Old and New Testaments are to be read, interpreted and understood as the word of God, there must be a flow-on effect as we listen to God speaking into the way we live inwardly and outwardly, collectively and individually.

It is here that the risk is no longer a risk but a guarantee of rejection from the world. If we stand for Christ exclusively, without carefully selecting which sections of Scripture we agree with and disregarding what remains, we will stand apart from the world. The divisiveness that Christ spoke about is not the result of his intention to destroy relationships but rather the result of his loving call for us to stand apart from the world in truth, so that we may live in his saving grace.

When what is being normalised in society lies in contradiction to the teachings of Christ, what will we do? When issues associated with injustice, sexuality, education, politics and religion confront us, where will we turn for answers? To make this even more difficult, the institutional church too often creates confusion that leads to divisiveness by conforming to the pressures of the surrounding culture, trading the rock of Christ for the sandy foundation of the world.

As the seasons of life continue to change, bringing new and recycled issues before us, we need to remember that our responses do involve risks. How do we weigh up those risks and what are the costs? It may just come down to some heated discussion, but it might also become the tipping point between truth, life and death.

The good news, however, is that the human right to life found in Christ alone is a right that cannot be taken away – even if it becomes politically incorrect, even in death.

Free at last

As we saw earlier in this book, no person is exempt when it comes to experiencing the struggles of life, and certainly no one can escape from themselves. The question was asked, 'Isn't it true that wherever you go, wherever you try to hide, there you will be?' The older one becomes, the more this reality will have set in and left its mark. Perhaps this is why we so often see that greener grass on the far side of the hill, only to find it ruined shortly after arrival by the dragging shackles of the 'self'. This is why the Scriptures teach us that we must die to self in order that we may live.

I have been crucified with Christ and I no longer live, but

Christ lives in me. The life I live now in the body, I live by faith in the Son of God, who loved me and gave himself for me' (Gal 2:20).

When life appears as a vast ocean in which we struggle to stay afloat, how comforting it is to feel a solid foundation under our feet. The waves may continue to envelop us in their wild fury, but the rock on which we stand holds us tall and steady in the white wash; our emerging faces finding comfort in the warm glow of the sunshine above. On Christ the solid rock we stand, this rock being a foundation of truth eternally anchored in God. This truth – God's enduring, unchanging truth – cannot be moved or broken. Rest and salvation are available for the exhausted water treader, being pulled every which way by the currents of life, trying desperately to maintain control by their own strength.

Surely, this is the truth of which Martin Luther King spoke as he powerfully preached:

'So if the Son [Christ] sets you free, you will be free indeed' *(Jn 8:36).*

It is the reality of who we are in Christ that has the power to set us free from any situation in which we may find ourselves as we come to the realisation that he is with us in all circumstances. There is nothing that can be done to us that can put an end to this reality. The world and even death have been defeated. When Jesus uttered his final words before giving up his spirit on the cross, he confirmed, *'It is finished'* (Jn 19:30). The word 'finished' in this part of Scripture means 'paid in full'.

The apostle Paul truly understood the power of hope in Christ as he often suffered for his faith. It is for this reason we can be encouraged by his words:

> *Therefore we do not lose heart. Though outwardly we are wasting away, yet inwardly we are being renewed day by day. For our light and momentary troubles are achieving for us an eternal glory that far outweighs them all. So we fix our eyes not on what is seen, but on what is unseen, since what is seen is temporary, but what is unseen is eternal' (2 Cor 4:16–18).*

While the unrelenting pressures of this life may not make diamonds out of us, we have something immeasurably more valuable than any precious jewel – the chance to really live for something infinitely bigger than ourselves. Here we find the hope and freedom we all long for.

Imprinting God

If true freedom is found in becoming more Christlike and living for something far greater than ourselves, how is this achieved?

'If any of you lacks wisdom, you should ask God, who gives generously to all without finding fault, and it will be given to you' (Jas 1:5).

If we understand wisdom to be the ability to make good use of knowledge and to recognise right from wrong, it would be safe to say that the path to wisdom is lined with an overwhelming amount of advice on where to find it.

Consider Plato's Symposium:

> Then Socrates sat down, and said, 'How fine it would be, Agathon, if wisdom were a sort of thing that could flow out of the one of us who is fuller into him who is emptier, by our mere contact with each other, as water flows through wool from the fuller cup into the emptier'.[5]

The question we might ask ourselves, then, is, 'What will be the source of the wisdom filling our cup?'

While the current trend in the Western world is to see wisdom subjectively and to gather it from an assortment of proclaimed truths that appeal to the individual, how can we ensure we are receiving our wisdom from the true source?

Firstly, when viewing the cosmos through a God-focused lens, you will find there are lessons to be learnt almost everywhere you turn. Personally, I learn a great deal by making connections between the natural world and the deeper truths

---

5 Plato's Symposium was a philosophical text by Plato written in 385–370 BC.

of life. The myth of scientific and Christian truth being in conflict comes across to me as bizarre – in fact, the opposite of what is true, as scientific ideas can provide powerful answers to questions relating to wisdom and how to become more Christlike.

Who would have thought we could learn about how to live for Christ by studying the behaviour of newly hatched goslings, for example? This may sound strange, but stay with me here. A famous study conducted by scientist Konrad Lorenz led to the understanding of a process called 'imprinting'.[6] Lorenz divided a clutch of graylag goose eggs, leaving some with the mother and placing the rest in an incubator. Those that hatched with the mother showed normal goose behaviour, following her about and learning from her until their coming of age. The goslings that hatched in the incubator were first exposed to the researcher and from that day on steadfastly followed Lorenz, demonstrating no recognition of their true mother or other adults of their own species. In a nutshell, this demonstrates how imprinting works in the animal kingdom.

As people who have been purposefully created to live in relationship with our Creator, we must ensure that we go through a process of imprinting with God as our focus. There are many potential influencers who seek our attention but only one who truly knows and cares about who we are, what we need and why we are here. This is what Jesus means when he teaches:

> 'When he [the Good Shepherd] has bought out all his own,
> he goes on ahead of them, and his sheep follow him because
> they know his voice. But they will never follow a stranger;
> in fact, they will run away from him because they do not
> recognise a stranger's voice' (Jn 10:4–5).

But how can God be the object of our imprinting, particularly as he is incomprehensible and often shrouded in

---

6 Neil A. Campbell, *Biology*, 2nd edn, Benjamin/Cummings, Redwood City CA, 1990, p. 1146.

mystery – and we're not goslings but relatively complex human beings? Obviously from a human perspective, much of what we have learnt from the day we were born has been influenced by our parents or those closest to us. The idea of imprinting by focusing on what God has revealed to us can only be understood in terms of our spiritual rebirth. From the moment we die to our old self and are spiritually reborn in Christ, we are to look to him, follow his voice and learn from his ways. If our imprinting is not based on Christ, make no mistake; we will imprint on alternatives. And the world offers us plenty of alternatives to choose from.

It is here that we need to come to terms with our inability to personally bring about any spiritual rebirth. And as the saying goes, there is no such thing as the evolution of the human spirit. We just can't change ourselves to become right with God. Rather, we can only acknowledge that our ability to turn to Christ – contradictory to our fallen nature – lies solely in the transforming power of God.

It is solely through the transforming work of the Holy Spirit that we are able to recognise Christ for who he is and the truth that exists in his words.

> *He was in the world, and though the world was made through him, the world did not recognise him. He came to that which was his own, but his own did not receive him. Yet to all who did receive him, to those who believed in his name, he gave the right to become children of God – children born not of natural descent, nor of human decision or a husband's will, but born of God (Jn 1:10–13).*

For God to be the subject of our imprinting we must, from the moment our eyes are opened, focus on Christ, as he is God revealed. As Luther once suggested, we should flee from the hidden God and look to God as revealed in Christ.[7] This is why the Scriptures say:

---

[7] Bayer, *Martin Luther's Theology*, p. 11.

> *We know also that the Son of God has come and has given us understanding, so that we may know him who is true. And we are in him who is true by being in his Son Jesus Christ. He is the true God and eternal life (1 Jn 5:20).*

In the animal kingdom, imprinting has been found to be crucial to the survival of individuals of certain species as they learn how to survive in their environment. Unlike those in the animal kingdom, relying on critical moments in the early stages of their lives to learn what is needed, those who belong to Christ do not depend on the laws of nature and key imprinting moments critical to the survival of the fittest. God has come to us; his Spirit works within us and guides us in truth as his ways are imprinted on our hearts. It's all in God's time and we are in his hands.

> *'Come to me, all you who are weary and burdened, and I will give you rest. Take my yoke upon you and learn from me, for I am gentle and humble in heart, and you will find rest for your souls. For my yoke is easy and my burden is light' (Mt 11:28–30).*

As the Holy Spirit makes it clear to us as to whom we belong, we become free to follow Christ as he reveals himself to us, prayerfully seeking to be transformed to be more like him each day. Ultimately, our eternal lives depend on him.

Walking with God

How remarkable it is to comprehend that each one of us was created to reflect God's glory, purposefully crafted in his image. Nothing else could be more important in life than living in communion with the one who knows us better than we know ourselves.

People reflect God in so many ways – and not always as predicted or expected. Several years ago, I once attended an Anglican church in which the senior minister left me with a simple, yet lasting, insight. Each morning he would get up before sunrise and spend time walking quietly, just himself and his Maker, listening, reflecting, praying and enjoying time out of the world's insanity.

Walking with God in this way is by no means a new concept, but in the crazy world in which we live, I suspect it is a dying or at least a fading practice. A perhaps lesser-known biblical character, Enoch, a member of Adam's family, knew this well. Through him, Scripture provides us with a way of deepening our relationship with God.

Altogether, Enoch lived a total of 365 years. Enoch walked faithfully with God; then he was no more, because God took him away (Gen 5:23–24).

God took Enoch! What this infers is that among the vast numbers of people who have lived on the Earth, only two never died according to Scripture, one being Enoch. Why? What is it about Enoch that separated him from the pack, and what can we learn from his ways?

It has been suggested that God and Enoch were in the habit of taking a long walk together every day, and that one day, God said to his companion, 'Why go home? Come all the way with Me'. And so it was that God took Enoch directly to live in his presence. While this may or may not be true, there is certainly wisdom associated with the way Enoch spent his earthly life.

While we shouldn't place our hope in sharing Enoch's direct assumption into God's presence, we followers of Christ can learn a lot from the way of Enoch. Here we find a man of outstanding sanctity who enjoyed intimate fellowship with God. It has also been suggested that the example of Enoch's assumption played a part in the origin of Jewish hope for life with God beyond death, an assurance now made clear in what has been achieved through Christ in his death and resurrection.

As we find ourselves inspired by the life of Enoch, we come to see the development of a great faith, one that was built over time, strengthened continually in the presence of the Heavenly Father.

> *By faith Enoch was taken from this life, so that he did not experience death; he could not be found, because God had taken him away. For before he was taken, he was commended as one who pleased God. And without faith it is impossible to please God, because anyone who comes to him must believe that he exists and that he rewards those who earnestly seek him (Heb 11:5-6).*

As we have seen throughout this book, along with the gift of the human mind's ability to reason, faith in God is also a gift. Our understanding of the gift of faith cannot be separated from our understanding of God's grace, in that we as people can do nothing to earn it. We can therefore only receive it with joyful and open arms as we embark on our journey to know God more deeply.

The gift of grace, received by faith, has the power to take us beyond the foolishness of human reason and philosophy alone. Luther understood this well, a concept that paved the way to a reformation that would change the world. Oswald Bayer, in reflecting on Luther's thoughts, suggests:

> *The image of God for the human being consists in the fact that the individual is the representative of God and is the one responsible for carrying out his mandates here on earth. Whoever is not satisfied with being an instrument of God and with being one who carries out his mandates destroys and misdirects the proper way to act in the image of God by glorifying himself instead, wrongly applying what was promised to him – the ability to reason using language.*[8]

Surely Enoch, because he pleased God, must have had a strong understanding of what it truly means to live as fully human, created in God's image and living to glorify his Creator.

It would make sense to ask at this point, 'What is this faith that Enoch and followers of Christ identify with?' It is the gift of being able to hear the gospel message and respond to what

8 Ibid., p. 159.

has been finished once and for all through Christ in his death and resurrection. It is the recognition of the reality of who God is and who we are as his creation.

We would all do well to learn from the way of Enoch, walking closely with God, closing our ears to Sinatra's words of 'I did it my way', and instead living as God intended: by faith in his grace. Perhaps a good place to embark on this journey is through reflection on the following poem:

Grace Story

You've always been there
You watched the pendulum of time unwind
Before the bells could sing their chime
Our Christ-bearing image forged within your mind
A revelation intimately signed
Creation's gift of breath and beauty intertwined
But breaking your heart, human sin denied
The true place of creatures and of God only divine
Yet in grace Father, Son and Spirit cried
"Let our perfect love shine it's Christmas light!"
In Christ humanity can truly be justified
As Satan's skull is crushed forever from life
Sadness and every tear will be wiped from their eyes
Now eternally loved and sanctified
In the heavenly dimensions of God his sheep will reside
In fields of gold, beholding the Tree of Life.

6. Time, Glory and a Final Call to Wisdom

What is it that we find when we truly seek to know God? Can we, in reality, know God?

These are the big questions that have directed the journey we've taken throughout this book. It is my hope that you have been challenged to form deep inner responses to these questions and that you will continue in your pursuit for the truth about who God is and who we are long after the final page of this book. Until then, I'd like to leave you with some final thoughts.

It's Father time

With every beat of our heart, with every tick of the clock, the time we have in this life edges closer to the finish line. If nothing else, this realisation should have us thinking about what it all means, this life that we've been given.

Common to Western cultures is a particular relationship with time. We strap it to our wrists; we hang it on our walls; it stares us in the face at every turn as we attempt to micromanage our days. We dare not let it out of our sight for fear of losing track.

As people so often do when it comes to making sense of life, things that are abstract or incomprehensible are reformed to reflect something more acceptable. They are moulded or created into something that better reflects finite human thinking. Hence time has come to be depicted by the character 'Father Time', an elderly bearded man with wings.

Regular human beings can only perceive what exists in four dimensions – one being time. The dimension of time leads to many questions, causing us much philosophical angst as we journey through life.

I can still hear the voice of my high school headmaster trying to impart his knowledge based on life experience. 'If only we could put an old head on your young shoulders, you could all be saved from learning things the hard way.' The youth rarely heed this advice, yet ironically continue to hand it over years down the track to the next generation.

How often do we hear lyrics that yearn for the ability to control time? After all, isn't this exactly what people seek, to control everything for their own purposes? When the Rolling Stones once suggested that time was on our side, they probably weren't reciting popular opinion. It's more probable for individuals to relate to Cher in her wish to turn back time! Perhaps one of the songs that speaks most deeply to our lives comes from the Australian band Powderfinger. In a song titled *These Days*, they speak of the relentless creeping hand of time and its command, lamenting over the realisation that life had turned out nothing like they had planned.[1]

And isn't this the case for so many of us? I suspect that the moment our older, experienced head sits firmly attached to our older body, we start to reflect on what might have been if we'd only done things differently. If only the shackles of time could be loosened, and we could have just one more roll of the dice.

> But the day comes when you're lying in the bath and you notice you are thirty-nine and that the way you're living bares scarcely any resemblance to what you thought you always wanted, and yet, you realize you got there by a long series of choices.[2]

The writer of Ecclesiastes made it his mission in life to try out everything under the sun, but concluded all to be

1 Jon Coghill, John Collins, Bernard Fanning, Ian Haug, Darren Middleton, *These Days*, Universal Music, 1999. From the album: *Odyssey Number Five.*
2 Timothy Keller, *Making Sense of God*, Hodder and Stoughton, London, 2016, p. 85. This quote used in Keller's book was originally a quote from *Fargo,* Season 2, Episode 10. See http://www.springfieldspringfield.co.uk/view_episode_scripts.php?tv-show=fargo-2014&episode=s02e10.

meaningless and warns those who are young that time has us all in its grip; life should not be wasted.

'Remember your Creator in the days of your youth, before the days of trouble come and the years approach when you will say, "I find no pleasure in them"' (Eccl 12:1).

In this scientific age, most people would not take seriously the idea of time having any link to a god, let alone *the* God. But can God really be removed from this concept without losing real perspective on how we are to relate to time and to God himself? And if God is the creator of all things, unbounded by time, then wouldn't that make time simply another aspect of creation with a beginning and an end?

Without God and the hope that exists in his grace, life in the rear-view mirror can sometimes appear meaningless or plunge us into a pool of regret. Our hope in Christ should remind us that the keys to the shackles of time are not in the hands of Father Time, but rather in the hands of the one who created time in the beginning. He will bring time to an end – and with it, the consequences of the poor decisions that seem to hold us to ransom each day. If our lives are really like sands through the hourglass, that hourglass has been given an expiry date. Christ has promised to set us free from the decay of this cursed life. Those who belong to him will no longer feel the need to dwell on the past but will live in his presence eternally in the absence of time and its command.

To overcome the temptation to look constantly into the rear-view mirror of life – as Lot's wife did when she was transformed into a pillar of salt – is a difficult thing. It goes against our natural way of thinking and in fact our tendency to focus on ourselves rather than on Christ. As we remind ourselves about who we belong to and the truth about time, perhaps we can join with the psalmist, who prays:

Show me, O Lord, my life's end and the number of my days; let me know how fleeting is my life. You have made my days a mere handbreadth; the span of my years is nothing before you. Everyone is but a breath (Ps 39:4–5).

Glory days

There is no denying it. It cannot be overstated. We have a short amount of time on this earth and an even shorter amount of time to reflect on what counts. We all need to ask ourselves the question, 'Are we here to create glory days for ourselves, or are we here to bring glory to our God?' While striving for greatness is often held as the pinnacle of Western living, it's a question of who we seek to glorify in the things we strive to achieve. God has equipped us with a vast array of gifts and abilities, but these can be used to either glorify ourselves or to glorify our Creator.

Surely, as followers of Christ, we are to clothe ourselves with the attitude of the psalmist in Psalm 115:1, who declares:

'Not to us, Lord, not to us but to your name be the glory, because of your love and faithfulness.'

When it comes to his own glorification, Jesus' way of being is very much tied to the nature of the Trinity and his relationship within it. As Christians, we need to grasp the importance of the perfect loving relationship between the Father, the Son and the Holy Spirit, so as to comprehend our purpose in glorifying God to all of the world, in all that we do. Jesus makes this clear when he prays for himself:

> *'Father, the hour has come. Glorify your Son, that your Son may glorify you. For you granted him authority over all people that he might give eternal life to all those you have given him. Now this is eternal life: that they know you, the only true God, and Jesus Christ, whom you have sent. I have brought you glory on earth by finishing the work you gave me to do. And now, Father, glorify me in your presence with the glory I had with you before the world began' (Jn 17:1–5).*

When we place ourselves firmly in the house of the living

God, immovably immersing ourselves in grace, we can become transformed in a way that brings glory to God, reflecting his glory into the world as we strive to live as he desires.

It's not that Christ needs us to bring glory to himself or to the Father; rather, it's that we who have been called to him feel compelled to acknowledge who he is and who we are in relation to him. Equipped with a knowledge of the reality of Christ, the focus of how we live should narrow in on bringing glory not to ourselves but to the one to whom glory belongs. After all, Jesus once said that if the people were to become silent in praising him, the stones themselves would cry out, for his glory will not be contained.[3]

Humankind has achieved so many great things and overcome so many immense challenges throughout history. We are constantly in awe of what we can achieve as we continue to build on the knowledge of our forebears. We've not only put a person on the moon but also explored the depths of space, mapping out a universe so vast and complex, it boggles the mind. We continually break records in the sporting arena and improve what the body can achieve through advances in nutrition and biomechanics. We have learned to stop many deadly diseases in their tracks and operate on delicate organs such as the brain using high-tech equipment. We've learned to harness the energy of nature, gradually creating more effective, sustainable forms of energy to combat climate change. The list could certainly go on. There is no question about the greatness of human potential; the question is simply about intentions. Will the goal of our potential be to achieve personal glory or, as Scottish runner Eric Liddell did in his athletics career, to bring glory to God in all that we achieve? For to bring glory to our Creator in this way is to play our part in the renewing of a broken world.

N.T. Wright, in his book *Simply Christian*, provides us with

---

3 See Luke 19:40.

the following insight:

> But new creation has already begun. The sun has begun to rise. Christians are called to leave behind, in the tomb of Jesus Christ, all that belongs to the brokenness and incompleteness of the present world. It is time, in the power of the Spirit, to take up our proper role, our fully human role, as agents, heralds and stewards of the new day that is dawning.[4]

Let us then embrace our personalised set of gifts, talents and opportunities by investing them securely in Christ, by bringing 'glory days' to the one to whom they ultimately belong. May grace then be perfected in the glory of God.

A final call to wisdom

There can be nothing more important than a life rooted in the eternal truth of Christ. While this book barely skims the surface of what can be said in answer to the big questions of who we are and who God is, I hope that your thirst for knowledge and truth has been awakened and that your future will be one that has the assurance of a life with God.

The French mathematician, physicist and religious thinker of the seventeenth century, Blaise Pascal, put human reason and faith into a well-balanced perspective. Pascal suggested that it is a mistake to trust in reason alone but also to despise reason and what it has to offer.[5] In other words, he denounced the idea of making humanity 'the measure of all things', while at the same time confronting thinkers who become ignorant of human nature and reflection.

For Martin Luther, the issue of how to approach reason lay in conceptualising the right way to interact with knowledge. Whoever has let himself become a fool because of the message of the cross does not seek to discover the nature of his existence

---

4 Tom Wright, *Simply Christian*, SPCK, London, 2006, p. 202.
5 Chapman, *Case for Christianity*, p. 169.

through philosophical reasoning. He has been set free from that type of thinking.[6]

Christianity will never be proven by reason alone. For as we have seen, if reason alone could explain the reality of God, then faith would become obsolete. Louis Berkhof expresses beautifully the relationship between reason and faith:

> The Christian accepts the truth of the existence of God by faith. But this faith is not a blind faith, but a faith that is based on evidence, and the evidence is found primarily in Scripture as the inspired Word of God, and secondarily in God's revelation in nature. Scriptural proof on this point does not come to us in the form of an explicit declaration, and much less in the form of a logical argument.[7]

Perhaps this is why effective Christian apologetics involves more than words. Reflecting Christ's love and truth, and bearing his image as he intends, provides an argument for God that is impossible to refute.

It only takes the merest opening of our eyes and minds to see that there are things in this world that are clearly not right. To live a life of blissful ignorance is not what we have been called to do. We have been personally created for a far higher purpose. When Paul encouraged us to be fools for Christ, he did not mean us to act as fools but rather to live a life for Christ, a life that would appear foolish to those who remain in worship of themselves. In the words of the wisest man to ever have lived, King Solomon:

> *Wisdom will save you from the ways of wicked men, from men whose words are perverse, who have left the straight paths to walk in dark ways, who delight in doing wrong and rejoice in the perverseness of evil, whose paths are crooked and who are devious in their ways (Prov 2:12–15).*

---

6 Bayer, *Martin Luther's Theology*, pp. 161–2.
7 Berkhof, *Systematic Theology*, p. 21.

When it comes to living a life of purpose, a life that has eternal meaning, surely it has to be a life immersed in the wisdom of Christ. We cannot expect to know how we should live if our hearts and minds are being diverted this way and that by the endless voices of those who sit apart from God's truth. When it comes to understanding the world's ongoing problems and issues, we Christians need to seek wisdom from the eternal King, whose knowledge far outweighs the futile thinking of finite minds.

Let us be encouraged to grow deeper in truth and wisdom, knowing God and knowing ourselves. Let us listen to his voice as we read his word and be guided by his spirit. Let us learn to discern the ways of Christ in a world that rarely bends its knee before the one who holds the keys to life.

This is life beyond the fish sticker.

My son, do not let wisdom and understanding out of your sight, preserve sound judgement and discretion; they will be life for you, an ornament to grace your neck. Then you will go on your way in safety, and your foot will not stumble (Prov 3:21–23).